Do the
RIGHT
Thing

Do the RIGHT Thing

The People's Economist Speaks

Walter E. Williams

HOOVER INSTITUTION PRESS
STANFORD UNIVERSITY, STANFORD, CALIFORNIA

Hoover Press Publication No. 430

First printing, 1995

01 00 99 98 97 96 95   9 8 7 6 5 4 3 2 1

Manufactured in the United States of America
The paper used in this publication meets the minimum requirements of American National Standard for Information Services—Permanence of Paper for Printed Library Materials, ANSI Z39.48-1984.

Library of Congress Cataloging-in-Publication Data

Williams, Walter E. (Walter Edward), 1936–
    Do the right thing: the people's economist speaks /
Walter E. Williams
        p. cm.—(Hoover Press publications: 430)
        ISBN 0-8179-9382-7 (pbk.)
        1. United States—Social policy. 2. United States—Politics and government—1989– 3. United States—Economic policy. I. Title
HN59.2.W527   1995   95–20174
361.6'1—dc20   CIP

CONTENTS

PREFACE

Regardless of whose sensibilities are offended, I do not hesitate to call things as I see them. Why? Because I care about our country and fear for its future as a free and prosperous nation. I address that concern by showing my fellow Americans how their well-intended actions and demands often constitute an assault on liberty and hence the supremacy of the individual. Worse yet, they often produce horrible unintended consequences. The major vehicle for this dialogue with my fellow citizens is my weekly column, which has been nationally syndicated for nearly fifteen years.

The subject matter of my columns covers the spectrum from government encroachment on our liberties to education and race discrimination. The underlying theme—protest, diatribe, call it what you will—is that institutions and actions fostering peaceable, voluntary exchange are moral. Those supporting coercion and control over individuals are immoral. There is nothing strange or unusual about these values; for the most part, they are articulated by most Americans. Indeed, they are the staple of all Fourth of July speeches and served as the moral anchor for our Declaration of Independence and our Constitution. The biggest difference between me and many of my fellow Americans is that I want liberty not only for myself but for others as well.

At the root of my values system is the principle of natural law as expounded by philosophers like John Locke and William Blackstone and adopted by early American notables such as Thomas Jefferson, James Madison, George Mason, Patrick Henry, and Thomas Paine, among others, and captured so simply, elegantly, and compellingly in our Declaration of Independence in the phrase "We hold these truths to be self-evident, that all men are created equal, that they are endowed by their Creator with certain unalienable rights, that among these are Life, Liberty and the Pursuit of Happiness."

The first principle of natural law holds that each person owns himself. In the state of nature, without government, all people are free and equal *but* insecure. That insecurity derives from the fact that other people may not respect our self-ownership rights and, through intimidation, threats, and coercion, wrongly confiscate our property and violate our persons.

Because of this insecurity, people form governments granting them certain limited powers. For example, in the state of nature, we all have the right to protect ourselves, family, and property from encroachment by others. When our rights to life, liberty, and property are violated, we have the right to be prosecutor, judge, jury, and, if need be, executioner. When we form governments, we grant these rights to the state in exchange for the guarantee that the state will perform these security functions. We give up only the rights necessary for government to perform its only function—protecting our security.

Through numerous successful attacks, private property and individual liberty are mere skeletons of their past. Thomas Jefferson anticipated this, saying, "The natural progress of things is for government to gain ground and for liberty to yield." An easy measure of how government is gaining ground is to look at the time spent earning money for which we have no claim. The average taxpayers works from January 1 to May 6 to pay federal, state, and local taxes. Each year we work a day or two longer to satisfy government. We should not forget that a working definition of slavery is that one works all year and has no claim to the fruits of his toil.

Liberty is threatened today not because of its failure but, somewhat ironically, because of its success. Liberty's counterpart in the economic arena, free markets, has been so successful in eliminating traditional problems like disease, pestilence, hunger, and gross poverty that all other human problems appear both unbearable and inexcusable.

The desire by many Americans to eliminate the so-called unbearable and inexcusable problems has led us astray from those basic ideals and principles on which our prosperous country was built. In the name of other ideals, such as equality of income, sex and race balance, orderly markets, consumer protection, energy conservation, and environmentalism, just to name a few, we have abandoned many personal freedoms. As a result of widespread control by government in an effort to achieve these so-called higher objectives, people have been subordinated to the point where considerations of personal freedom are but secondary or tertiary matters. The ultimate end to this process is totalitarianism, which is no more than a reduced form of servitude.

The primary justification for the attack on liberty and economic freedom can be found in people's desire for government to do good. We say government should care for the poor, the disadvantaged, the elderly, failing businesses, college students, and many other "deserving" segments of our society. However, we must recognize government has no resources of its own; in other words, members of Congress and senators are not spending their *own* money for the programs. Furthermore, there's no tooth fairy or Santa Claus who gives them the resources. The recognition that government does not have any resources of its own forces us to recognize that the only way that the government can give one American one dollar is to confiscate it from another American through intimidation, threats, and coercion.

Americans support government doing things that, if done by a private person, they would condemn as common thievery. For example, if I used force to take what rightfully belongs to one person and gave it to another who was in need, most would condemn my actions as those of a common thief. If we accept that privately confiscating the property of one, and giving it to another to whom it does not belong is immoral, is it any less so when done collectively, through government? I think not. Despicable acts like theft, rape, and murder, which are clearly an affront to human rights when done privately, do not become moral simply because of legal sanctions or majority consent.

Writing syndicated columns has given me several important benefits. First, it has taught me how to translate potentially complex topics in economics in ways the average person can readily understand. I take great pride in this accomplishment, for it was Professor Armen Alchian, one of my tenacious mentors at the University of California at Los Angeles, where I took my Ph.D., who told me that the true test of whether someone really understands his subject is whether he can explain it to someone who knows nothing about it. Second, I love teaching, and my column affords me the opportunity to extend my classroom beyond the confines of brick and mortar at George Mason University, where I teach economics. Lastly, in the course of writing columns, I have encountered valuable reader response. Some of it was scolding and taught me to sharpen my tools of discourse and explain things more clearly. Some of the response gave me rich information about people's lives or events that I could have never otherwise known.

The columns included in this collection were selected from the years 1990 through 1994. About 120 newspapers across the United States have published them. Previously published collections of my columns appeared in book form under the titles of *America: A Minority View* and *All It Takes Is Guts*.

ACKNOWLEDGMENTS

The fact that one's status at birth does not necessarily determine one's status in later life is something uniquely American. Like many of my fellow Americans I have benefited from the kind of socioeconomic mobility long a part of our tradition. When one travels that long road from a North Philadelphia housing project to being a professor of economics and a nationally syndicated columnist, among other achievements, there is no way he can sit back and say, "I did it all by myself."

Much of the credit for what I have achieved belongs to a mother who, having been abandoned by her husband, raised two children by herself through difficult times. She is the one who gave me a spirit of rebelliousness, taught me hard lessons about independence and discipline, and always reminded my sister and me, "We may have a beer pocketbook, but we have champagne tastes."

In 1960 I was fortunate enough to choose a wife who not only shared my vision of what we needed to do to make it out of the slums of North Philadelphia but shouldered a lot of that burden, working full time while I attended college. We are still lovers and friends, and she is still my main cheerleader. And on top of all that she's graciously shared my love for her with a beautiful and charming daughter.

It must have been an act of Providence that enabled me to have teachers in high school and professors in college who didn't give a damn about what color I was and held me accountable to high standards. In that respect I consider myself fortunate to have had virtually all my education before it became fashionable for white people to like black people. That meant that my educators were free to challenge whatever nonsense I uttered without fear of accusations of racism. That is not so true in today's era of "enlightened" racial relationships. And such sensitivity and political correctness deprives many black students of honest assessments of their academic work.

Acknowledgment must also go to friends and colleagues, plus detractors, who gave me valuable criticism. A word of thanks and appreciation also goes to the Olin Foundation, which has graciously funded my John M. Olin Distinguished Professorship at George Mason University for well over a decade. The financial assistance has made it possible for me to engage in many activities beyond those of the traditional professor. I also wish to express gratitude to the Heritage Foundation for getting me started in the syndication business in 1980 through their then newly launched Heritage Features Syndicate. In 1991, in a friendly buyout, Creators Syndicate took over my column with no perceptible change in congeniality or assistance.

Finally, a word of acknowledgment must go to Kathy Spolarich, my secretary/assistant, who has been invaluable in running down information, typing innumerable drafts, catching my mistakes in grammar, managing my schedule, and being cheerful about it all to boot.

RACE & SEX

Issues surrounding race have dogged our nation since its inception. During the civil rights battles of the 1950s and 1960s, it would not have been overly optimistic to expect that problems of race would have all but disappeared by the 1990s. Nonetheless, they remain with us, and often it appears that we are going backward rather than forward.

Part of the dilemma is the vision that sees the current problems black Americans face as civil rights problems. For all intents and purposes, the civil rights struggle is over and it is won. *Acknowledging that the civil rights struggle is over does not mean that there are not serious problems within a large segment of the black community. It simply means that the problems that remain* are not *civil rights problems.*

Black illegitimacy, which currently stands at 66 percent nationally, estimated to be 75 percent by the end of this century, is a devastating problem, but it is not a civil rights problem. The high rate of crime, which makes life unbearable for the overwhelmingly law-abiding majority of many black neighborhoods and makes economic progress all but impossible, is a major problem but not a civil rights problem. The grossly fraudulent education received by a majority of black students in government-owned schools is a major problem but, again, not a civil rights problem.

Recognizing that most problems affecting the black community are not civil rights problems would allow us to investigate and perhaps find other solutions. In other words, if poor-quality black education is seen as a civil rights problem, then its solutions are busing and getting more black administrators and teachers, more educational dollars, more

1

black superintendents of schools, more black mayors, and more repre-
sentation on city councils. All those measures have been tried and have
been dismal failures in terms of improving black education. In fact,
black security, black socioeconomic progress, and black education are
the worst in the very cities where a black is the mayor, where blacks
dominate the city council, where a black is chief of police, and where a
black is superintendent of schools.

In the columns that follow, I point out many of the myths and
tragedies about black life and present the argument that improvement
will come when we realize that solutions cannot be parachuted in from
Washington, D.C., and state capitals. The solutions must be produced
and managed at the local levels. It will take churches, fraternities and
sororities, Rotary Clubs, and grassroots organizations to rebuild fami-
lies and those institutions that were so valuable in the march from sla-
very to civil rights. In addition, a few columns address issues in sex
discrimination such as sex differences and whether women should be
in combat.

Civil Rights Visions

NOVEMBER 6, 1991

If you think politicians and the intellectual elite can be trusted, feast your
eyes on this agenda, which you won't hear about on the six o'clock news.

Senator Wyche Fowler (D-Ga.), with the cosponsorship of Senators
Daschle, Heflin, Sanford, Shelby, Harkin, Metzenbaum, and Inouye, has
introduced S.2881, which is titled the "Minority Farmers' Rights Act."
If enacted, it would require the secretary of agriculture to create a "National Minority Farmer and Land Registry containing the names of all
minority farmers and a legal description of their land holdings." The
new agency will be required to "establish policies and programs that
contribute to the expansion of such [a] land base." The bill also, "in the
case of agricultural land held or administered by the Department [of
Agriculture], requires such land owned by the United States to be used
to reverse the contraction of the minority agricultural land base."

The Fowler bill doesn't only call for farmland quotas, it goes further: "The secretary shall review minority participation compared to non-minority participation in all crop programs of the department on a state-by-state and county-by-county basis." It also requires the Department of Agriculture to "include specific numerical goals for increased training and promotion of the minority employees of the agencies and for the increased participation of minorities in the programs"; the department must also "establish a timetable for the achievement of the goals."

When the 1991 Civil Rights Act, which "read-my-lips" Bush promised to veto and has now agreed to support, becomes law, we are going to see volumes of quota policy like Senator Fowler's Minority Farmers' Rights Act.

Black farmers should be outraged by the act for at least two reasons. The act "encourage[s] any sale or transfer of any portion of the minority agricultural land base to other minority farmers," which means that when a black sells his land, he can only sell it to a black buyer. Simple economics says that the fewer the number of potential buyers, the lower the expected price. Therefore, the Minority Farmers' Rights Act will lower the value of all land held by blacks.

But there's a greater danger. When Franklin Roosevelt and Earl Warren were interning Japanese-Americans or when the Nazis were exterminating Jews, reliable information about who owned what by race would have been an invaluable tool. Now you say, "Williams, that can't happen here!" I hope not, but given present trends, it's not wise to dismiss it altogether.

But there's more on the quota front. University of Michigan president James Duderstadt said, "There is no quota system at the U-M," adding, "we've never had quotas." Duderstadt concluded, "We seek a student body composition that is reflective of the national composition." According to my colleague Thomas Sowell, we call that an "un-quota."

Here's part of a letter from the University of California at Los Angeles's (UCLA's) School of Law dean Michael D. Rappaport. "Dear Applicant: Your recent application to UCLA School of Law suggests that you may be a member of a minority group. If you would like the Admissions Committee to consider your ethnicity as part of your application, the Committee would appreciate it if you would elaborate on your ethnic background." How do you like them apples? I bet UCLA's catalog contains a statement such as, UCLA does not discriminate by race, sex, religion, or national origin. But UCLA can't top Penn State University's official policy, which pays any black student earning a C average a $580 cash bonus. Getting a B means a $1,160 bonus.

If we're going to prevent racial chaos in our country, decent Americans of all races must disavow and outlaw official and unofficial racist policy.

Building a Trojan Horse

November 20, 1991

Americans are following the path of pre-Nazi Germany; for that reason, we haven't heard the last of David Duke–type aspirants for high political office. Writing about Nazi Germany in his book *The Road to Serfdom*, Nobel laureate Friedrich Hayek said, "The supreme tragedy is still not seen that in Germany it was largely people of good will . . . who prepared the way for, if they did not actually create, the forces which now stand for everything they detest."

In the pursuit of rogue notions of "social justice," Germans completely abandoned principles of rule of law, private property, and limited government. They were only too willing to give up local authority and grant authoritarian rule to the central government, all of which provided the Trojan horse for Hitler. The essentials of Germany's scenario were duplicated in Russia and China and, as in Germany, resulted in tragedies of unspeakable proportions.

Americans are nowhere near the tyrannical regimes of Germany, Russia, and China, but if you ask, "Where are we heading?" it is toward tyranny and run-amok government rather than liberty. An essential ingredient of a tyrant's agenda is to exploit the problems and resentment of people. And here's where David Duke comes in. There is little anyone can do about the relatively small group of Americans who are out-and-out racists. In many ways, they can be safely ignored. What a David Duke must do is attract the interest of large numbers of whites who are not racists.

An effective way to capture their interest is to talk about the grossly unjust forms of affirmative action public policy. One doesn't have to be a racist to object to affirmative action programs that mandate that blacks who achieve lower employment test scores be hired or promoted over whites who achieve higher scores. You don't have to be a racist to resent seeing a black professor, Leonard Jeffries of the City University of New York, keep his job after having referred to whites as "ice people" and having publicly called the U.S. assistant secretary of education a "Texas Jew." White professors making comparatively minor transgressions have been censored, been fired, or had their classes canceled. If you're white and resentful of official racially discriminatory policy, who speaks for you? It's David Duke. Bush's signing the 1991 Civil Rights Act will help the David Dukes of the United States much more than it will help blacks.

Duke's companion campaign issues are welfare and crime, two other issues that can be used to create resentment. Blacks are by no means the most numerous recipients of welfare; neither do we commit the most crimes. But in terms of percentages, enough of us are on welfare and commit enough crimes so that a David Duke can retain plausibility by making welfare and crime race issues.

If we are appalled at Duke's political success, let us consider just how successful a Duke-type presidential candidate might be under the following scenario: Congress has created an economic nightmare. An important element of that nightmare is our official national debt of $3 trillion that is unofficially much closer to $6 trillion. The debt will be repudiated. That will mean severe economic chaos. When people are losing their jobs, savings, and homes in large numbers, I imagine a David Duke could be very successful at the national level. Like Hitler with the Jews, he would have a natural scapegoat—blacks and Hispanics.

Unless you are prepared to tell me that this is impossible in America, we'd better act quickly before it's too late. We shouldn't focus on Duke as much as on finding ways to stop creating kindling for racial arsonists.

Is Combat for Women?

JULY 24, 1991

Several members of Congress are pushing legislation to lift the ban on women in military combat positions. At the risk of being drawn and quartered in this age of "politically correct" thinking, I think women should not be in combat positions or in any job that has the remotest risk of being subject to combat. The military's task is to fight and win wars, not prove our commitment to sex equality.

The Heritage Foundation recently published an article, written by Robert H. Knight, on recent testimony by Colonel Patrick Toffler, director of West Point's Office of Institutional Research. Some physical training for both sexes has been eliminated at West Point or made easier so that women would not suffer an "adverse impact." Cadets no longer train in combat boots because women cadets suffer higher rates of injury. West Point males must do full pull-ups while females get by with "flex-arm hangs." Running with heavy weapons has been eliminated because it is "unrealistic and therefore inappropriate" to expect women to do it. In load-bearing tasks, 50 percent of the female cadets score lower than the bottom 5 percent of the men. West Point men are not as cardiovascularly fit nowadays because of physical training standards geared to women.

Physical differences between men and women are important to combat efficiency. Plus, there are important psychological differences. On psychological measures of competitiveness, aggressiveness, vindictiveness, and just plain meanness, men score much higher than women. Although an abundance of these characteristics may not make for a congenial tea and cookie gathering, they fit the bill if you're looking for people to kill, maim, destroy, and capture.

As in other congressional social agendas, honesty takes a backseat. During the Panama invasion, a female truck driver, taking troops into the combat zone, started crying. Another woman performing the same job also broke into tears. Both women were relieved of duty. After reporters learned of the incidents, the army "took pains to convey that the women had not disobeyed orders or been derelict in their duty," reports the *New Republic* (February 19, 1991). According to an army official quoted in the *Washington Post* on the matter, "They performed superbly." The point here is not to single out women—men crack up during combat too. The point is to show that gross lies, suppression of dissent, and intimidation are the strategy of those with a social mission.

Senator Barbara Mikulski (D-Md.) demanded an "attitude change" at the naval academy. Her committee calls for "immediate dismissal of senior officers who question the role of women in the military." The most recent academy report calls for combating the "widespread misperception that the academy's mission is to produce warriors and only warriors" and that the officers who "foster the opinion that women should not be midshipmen should be relieved." Male officers are unofficially warned that their career advancement will suffer if they dispute the official line that women in the military cause no problems and don't hamper military effectiveness.

"What's the beef, Williams?" you say. "Didn't we win the gulf war with women?" First of all, the gulf war was mostly a display of high-tech military hardware, the ground war was a 100-hour cakewalk, and the women, God bless them, were engaged in the less hazardous and less demanding roles of support.

Kindling for the Racial Bonfire

MAY 13, 1992

What can we make of David Duke picking up 55 percent of the white vote in Louisiana's gubernatorial election or Pat Buchanan using similar themes and dogging President Bush in several primaries? Although it's tempting to dismiss Duke supporters as racist, we might want to reconsider the premise when Buchanan achieves a modicum of political viability exploiting voter resentment against quotas, welfare, and foreigners.

Race has always been a problem in our country; we've always had, and still have, racists in America. Fortunately, racists have never been anywhere near a majority. Indeed, it was black people's appeal to the sense of morality and fair play of the nonracist majority that was partly responsible for the phenomenal, unprecedented success of a civil rights movement that saw a people once enslaved rise to enjoy full constitutional protections.

Within the last decade or so, we have seen a rise in racial conflict and resentment. Especially unsettling is that much of this resentment is among our youth on college campuses. The irony is that these youngsters may be the children or grandchildren of black and white people who marched arm in arm risking their lives on the back roads of Selma, Alabama, the streets of Montgomery and shared Martin Luther King's dream of racial equality.

Organizations once part of a proud struggle have now squandered their moral authority. They are little more than race hustlers championing a racial spoils system. They no longer seek fair play and a color-blind society; their agenda is one of group rights where quota is king and color blindness is viewed with contempt. Today's civil rights organizations differ only in degree, not in kind, from white racist organizations past and present.

Blame for the resurgence of racial resentment rests with otherwise decent people who tolerate and implement racist demands. Among these are college administrators who give in to black student demands for racially exclusive campus facilities or subsidize a black student union and intimidate a white student union and employers that have one set of performance standards for whites and another for blacks. Also to blame are union agreements where, should layoffs become necessary, higher-seniority whites are laid off before lower-seniority blacks in the name of racial balance and contract set-asides that harm small white businesses in order to benefit small black businesses.

As we stack up piles of combustible racial kindling, we should not be surprised to see racial arsonists come along to set it ablaze. Political appeal to America's racists is a no-win situation. For a racial arsonist to be successful, he has to be able to exploit what are seen as legitimate resentments of that nonracist majority. In other words, you don't have to be a racist to resent being laid off before someone who has less seniority. You don't have to be a racist to be offended by having to score 70 to pass an exam when a black passes with a 65.

If you are offended by these practices, who speaks for you? Does George Bush or Bill Clinton? The only politicians addressing your con-

cerns are the David Dukes and the Pat Buchanans. It is not likely that
Duke or Buchanan will make inroads of any significance this time
around. But with the 1991 Civil Rights Act mandating greater use of
quotas and the threat of financial upheaval in the not-too-distant future, don't be surprised to see racial resentment successfully exploited.
If that day comes, it will be decent Americans who paved the way.

Politically Correct Bean Counters

JANUARY 13, 1993

Clinton's eighteen-person cabinet consists of nine white men, four blacks,
four women, and two Hispanics. You say, "Hold it, Williams, nine plus
four plus four plus two equals nineteen! Can't you at least count?"

The problem is double counting. Where do we put Hazel O'Leary,
Clinton's appointee for secretary of energy, a black woman? Do we
count her as a woman or a black? Is race more important than sex for,
to use Clinton's phrase, America's "bean counters?" If O'Leary goes on
the black list, blacks are way ahead—being only 12 percent of the population but 22 percent of Clinton's cabinet. But if O'Leary goes on the
woman list, it cuts blacks to 16 percent of the cabinet and brings women
up to only 22 percent, far below their 51 percent of the general population. It's only white men, making up 50 percent of Clinton's cabinet,
who are proportionately represented.

You say, "What do you mean 'proportionately represented'? White
men aren't 50 percent of the population! They're overrepresented."

But don't complain; look at blacks. We're 12 percent of the population but 22 percent of Clinton's cabinet, if O'Leary goes on the black
list. Even Hispanics are overrepresented, being 11 percent of the cabinet but only 9 percent of the population.

You might ask how come, among America's four groups of people,
it's women who are grossly underrepresented? Patricia Schroeder (D-
Colo.) put her finger on it, saying, "This cabinet will look like America:
with men at the top." Schroeder's assessment may be right, and there's
a good reason for it. Clinton isn't afraid of women, and it's the women

of America's fault. If Clinton messes around with us blacks, he knows what we will do; we don't play. If you don't believe it, look at southwest Los Angeles, Watts, Detroit, and Chicago and watch what will happen to Hollywood if Spike Lee's *Malcolm X* doesn't win an Oscar. Hispanics have been known to act out as well, and everybody knows that white men can be megaviolent—just ask Saddam Hussein.

Nobody's afraid of women. Who's ever heard of women torching and looting a city? Hussein would have laughed in our faces had we sent a division of women to do battle with his elite palace guards. The policy recommendation for women who want to increase their percentages in future presidential cabinets is as plain as day: Women must adopt the successful tactics of minorities and men. Until women put the fear of God into men, like my wife has put into me, they'll always be underrepresented in presidential cabinets.

You say, "Okay, Williams, that's a marvelous analysis, but there are more than just four groups in America."

That's an issue best ignored. It adds too much complexity to the lives of pc/bcs (politically correct bean counters). Suppose there were a homosexual cabinet quota? There'd be a verification problem. How can you tell whether a person is really a homosexual or an imposter? After all, white people have been known to report that they're black in order to get in on a black quota.

There's another problem. Clinton can't go out and randomly round up white men and have a truly representative cabinet. After all there are different kinds of white men, Greek, Italian, Polish, Armenian, Irish, English, German, Swedish, and French white men who can't be lumped into one big happy family. If you don't believe me, ask a Croat how he feels about a Serb. Plus, there are great opportunities for ethnic misrepresentation: an English-American might fake being a Swede. To guard against racial misrepresentation, we must adopt what South Africa has discarded—a Population Registry Act, with a Racial Classification Appeal Board.

Racial Double Standards

FEBRUARY 10, 1993

America's intellectual elites, aided by the media, are bringing racial/ethnic chaos to our country. Part of this process is found in Jared Taylor's well-documented book *Paved with Good Intentions*. We've all heard of the 1986 Howard Beach incident in New York, where a bunch of bat-wielding whites brutally beat two black youths and sent another running to his death. This became national and international news. Three years later, a black was set on and shot in the Bensonhurst section of Brooklyn—again, nationally reported.

But here are some stories I bet you haven't heard. In 1989, a white man was badly beaten by a group of blacks in Cleveland. As he was lying in the street, a black got in the man's truck and ran over him to the cheers of the crowd. In January 1991, four blacks agreed to kill the first white person they saw. A Northeastern University student in Boston was unlucky enough to be the first; he was stabbed to death. In 1991, a black man was arrested for murdering seven white people. He explained the murders by "a deep-rooted hatred for white people."

Of course, this could be your standard news media's selective reporting of the news, but it could also be a result of their college training. Some universities, among them the University of Cincinnati, have student handbooks that say, and professors who teach, that blacks are incapable of racism. Therefore, media people see the Howard Beach and Bensonhurst incidents—where whites murdered and beat blacks—as racist and view situations where blacks do the same to whites as simply crimes.

The Reverend Jesse Jackson led the call for Cincinnati Reds owner Marge Schott's suspension for making racially derogatory remarks about blacks. In 1989, Gus Savage, a black congressman from Chicago, responded to a reporter: "I don't want to talk to you white motherf—s. F— you, you mother-f—ing a—hole white devils." Do you think Jesse called for censure of Gus Savage? Can you imagine the outrage if Jesse Helms made similar remarks to a black reporter? Then again, Brother JJ has a problem with racially derogatory remarks as well, having referred to New York as "hymie-town." In 1991, Dr. Khalid Muhammad gave a talk at Columbia University in which he referred to the school as "Columbia Jewniversity" and New York as "Jew York City" and advised that the blacks who attacked the Central Park jogger were in jail because of a "no-good, low-down, nasty white woman." Jesse didn't call for Muhammad's suspension. Jesse probably shares Stanford professor Charles Lawrence's view that speech codes should only protect "historical victim groups."

With Donna Shalala as head of Health and Human Services, ideas of the intellectual elite might become the law of the land. At her University of Wisconsin, a white student was suspended for addressing a black as "Shaka Zulu." However, when three white students objected to being called "rednecks," they were told that the word was not on the forbidden list and that no offense could be taken. At UCLA, a student newspaper editor was suspended for running a cartoon featuring a rooster who, when asked how he got into UCLA, replied, "affirmative action." However, when a UCLA minority student newspaper said that Europeans "do not possess the qualities of rational thought, generosity, and magnanimity," nothing happened.

There's a real question of how long we can remain a reasonably civil society in the wake of elite half-baked schemes that are tearing us apart. *Paved with Good Intentions* should be on everybody's bookshelf. Admittedly, it is tragic reading. But it's far better to know and do something about liberals tearing down our country before it's too late.

The Big Rip-Off

MAY 12, 1993

Americans have been sold a bill of goods. We have legitimate grievances about what's been happening in our cities and on matters of race, but we've been unfocused. And we're being readied to take it in the pockets again by social engineers who are little more than quacks, hustlers, and charlatans. Let's look at it.

In the wake of the Los Angeles riots, mayors, public employee unions, urban "scholars," many members of Congress, and other assorted urban hustlers tell us we need a $35 billion urban Marshall Plan to save our cities because, according to D.C. delegate Eleanor Holmes Norton, there's been "a massive federal disinvestment in the cities during the 1980s." However, *The Myth of America's Underfunded Cities*, written by Stephen Moore and Dean Stansel of the Washington-based Cato Institute, points out that since the late 1960s, the federal government has spend $2.5 trillion on urban renewal and poverty. That is the equivalent of twenty-five Marshall Plans, or, more interestingly, the 1986 value of all the financial assets of all our Fortune 500 companies and all our farmland.

We've listened to the counsel of people like Harvard University professor Kenneth Galbraith, who twenty-five years ago said there's nothing wrong with New York that doubling the city's budget wouldn't solve. Adjusted for inflation, the city's budget tripled between 1965 and 1990. By any measure, New York and other major metropolitan areas, which saw budgets double or triple during the period, are infinitely worse off now.

During President Reagan's tenure, direct federal aid to cities was cut by 50 percent. However, federal direct aid to poor people living in cities rose from $255 billion to $285 billion in real dollars during that period. In Bush's four years, social spending rose by 25 percent, the fastest increase in thirty years. Any reductions in direct federal aid to cities were more than offset by federal programs (education, training, social services, welfare, community development, etc.) for people who live there. Moreover, for every federal dollar lost, cities got 80 cents from the state.

What's the result? Cities in the steepest decline are those that receive the most federal aid, have the highest tax rate, and have the highest spending per capita. Cities spending the most on education have the poorest student academic performance. If a man from Mars asked you how to identify cities that spent the most money per capita, it would be easy. Just tell the guy to look for cities with the steepest decay and decline, greatest crime rates, greatest family breakdown, most rotten schools, and filthiest streets.

Not surprisingly, people in these cities (New York, Chicago, Philadelphia, Detroit, Baltimore, Cleveland, Washington, D.C.), like those in Third World countries, get out at their first opportunity. Liberals used to attribute the flight to racism—"white flight" to the suburbs.

Black people don't like mugging, drive-by shootings, or property destruction either. For the past two decades, black flight has exceeded white flight to the suburbs.

Too many inner-city problems are seen through a racial lens; they are not all that. They are human problems. If New York City were all white, paid school janitors an average of $57,000 a year (some make $80,000), gave public employees fifty-one days off a year, spent $6,500 per student to have only one-third graduate on time, if at all, and had punitive taxes, it would be a Third World white city. And if you guessed that the desire to do more boondoggling underlies the recent call for an urban Marshall Plan, go to the head of the class.

The Framers Tried

MAY 26, 1993

When expressing admiration for the wisdom of our Constitution's framers, I sometimes encounter derisive responses such as, "Some were slave owners," "They made blacks three-fifths of a person," and "They condoned slavery." Thus, the implied conclusion is that we shouldn't respect these dead white men. Let's evaluate this misinformation that's become a part of the regular curriculum in too many of today's high schools and colleges.

Thomas Jefferson's first draft of the Declaration of Independence charged that "[the king of Britain] has waged a cruel war against human nature itself, violating its most sacred rights of life and liberty in the persons of distant people who never offended him, captivating and carrying them into slavery in another hemisphere." In 1764, James Otis of Massachusetts said, "The colonists are by law of nature freeborn, as indeed all men are, white or black."

Other founders expressed similar antislavery sentiments. Thomas Paine: "And when the Almighty shall have blessed us and made us a people, then may our first gratitude be shown, by an act of continental legislation which shall put a stop to the importation of Negroes for sale, and in time procure their freedom." John Adams: "I have, through my whole life, held the practice of slavery in abhorrence." Benjamin Franklin: "Slavery is an atrocious debasement of human nature." George Washington: "There's not a man living who wishes more sincerely than I do, to see a plan adopted for the abolition of [slavery]." James Madison: "[Southern laws have] degraded slaves from the human rank. It was a barbarous policy." Alexander Hamilton: "Their [blacks'] natural faculties are probably as good as ours. The contempt we have been taught to entertain for the blacks makes us fancy many things that are neither founded in reason or experience." Jefferson, however, believed blacks were inferior but said, "Whatever may be the degree of talent it is no measure of their rights. Because Isaac Newton was superior to others in understanding, he is not therefore lord of the person or property of others."

In 1787, the framers of the Constitution were faced with a serious dilemma—a choice between union and disunion. Slavery opponents chose union. They felt slavery would continue with or without the Constitution. The question was whether there would be a future for liberty. It was slavery's opponents who succeeded in restricting the political power of the South by allowing them to count only three-fifths of their slave population in determining the number of congressional representatives. The three-fifths of a vote provision applied only to slaves, not to free blacks in either the North or the South.

You say, "Williams, I went to high school and college and didn't learn this; how do you know it?" It's not me but my friends who mail me all sorts of goodies. In this case, it was University of Dallas professor Thomas G. West's article, "Was the American Founding Unjust?" in *Principles*, a publication of the Claremont Institute's Salvatori Center in Claremont, California. Marshaling the truth is a vital defensive weapon in today's war against Americanism and traditional values. Politicians, news media, college professors, and leftists of other stripes are selling us lies and propaganda. To lay the groundwork for their increasingly successful attack on our Constitution, they must demean and criticize its authors. As Senator Joe Biden demonstrated during the Clarence Thomas hearings, the framers' ideas about natural law must be trivialized or they must be seen as racists.

The truth about our history is vital to the preservation of our liberty. If your high schooler or college kid is taking early American history, give them some facts they otherwise won't learn.

Government versus Civility

JULY 7, 1993

Let's create a list of offensive behaviors. My list would include loud belching and gaseous anal emissions, picking one's nose, strangers viewing *Penthouse* centerfolds in public, cursing at one's parents, and blaring car radios. Your list might include others. Here's the question: Which offensive behavior, if any, should be prohibited by law? If you don't think they should be prohibited, should they be legalized? For example, in the name of free speech, would you support the enactment of a statute reading that children may curse their parents?

The point is easy. The job of civil institutions, values, and customs is to keep undesirable behavior within tolerable limits. Civil institutions are family, churches, schools, neighborhood associations, and clubs. Customs and values are the codified religious "shalt nots" and Emily Post's rules of etiquette. No individual or group of individuals sat down and conjured up these institutions, values, and customs. They simply evolved as the received wisdom of ages on ages of people deciding what works best and what doesn't.

Out of conceit and arrogance, the elite use government to undermine and weaken civil institutions, values, and customs. As if needing to confirm their conceit and arrogance, the elite seek to replace what has worked with laws to control behavior formerly kept within tolerable limits through civil institutions, values, and customs.

For generations, boys were taught that certain kinds of behavior were not acceptable in the presence of women. They were taught courtesy, attentiveness, and not to use foul language, and assault was out of the question altogether, even if your face were slapped. Women were to be placed on a pedestal. These civilizing lessons made a lot of sense because of the awesome physical power difference between men and women. Similarly, there were codes of conduct taught girls. You didn't go unchaperoned to a man's room; you didn't let a guy go "too far" on the first date or two; you were told to always behave in a ladylike fashion.

For the last several decades, these values and customs, and the civil

institutions that fostered them, have been seen as archaic and unneces-
sarily inhibitive of fun. And they've been seen as impediments to the
social engineering agenda and ideology of society's elite that call for
women being declared equal to men.

Take the Mike Tyson case. The radical feminist variety of the arrogant elite thinks it's OK for women to throw caution to the wind, visit a
foul-talking man's hotel suite at two o'clock in the morning, and expect
no untoward consequences. Similarly, they think it's OK for female navy
officers, as in the Tailhook incident, to go braless in tank tops, mini-
skirts, and heels up to an all-male floor where a bunch of raucous sailors
are trying to drink all the booze in sight. The social engineers say we
shouldn't distinguish between men and women. Then they get into a huff
and whimper when "boys act like boys" and women can't cope.

There are many other examples of elite undermining of civil institutions. That's why we see disrespect for the rights and property of
others, family breakdown, teen pregnancy, high divorce rates, and other
indicators of social rot. My point is not that we shouldn't question civil
institutions, values, and customs. But we must not forget that they represent historical stores of wisdom passed on from one generation to
another. We'd better seriously examine their social role before we cast
them aside in favor of government regulation of behavior.

Is It Racism?

September 1, 1993

You're dressed and headed for work. Opening the garage, you find
yourself eye to eye with a full-grown tiger. What's your response? You'd
leave the area in great dispatch. That prediction is uninteresting, but
the reasons for your behavior aren't. Was your decision based on de-
tailed information about that particular tiger? Or was it based on information held about tiger folklore and behavior of other tigers? You
stereotyped that tiger. Instead of trying to see whether that tiger was
like others before you took action, you prejudged him.

On a Saturday morning in 1972, while picking up litter outside my house in Chevy Chase, Maryland, an exclusive neighborhood in the Washington, D.C., area, a white man approached and asked whether later I'd be interested in doing handy work at his house. I responded no because I'd be in the house working on my Ph.D. dissertation. The man was embarrassed and apologized profusely.

Months later, my wife's car was being repaired, and she went hitchhiking to the bus stop. A black lady, who turned out to be a domestic servant, picked her up. During the conversation, the lady asked, "Don't you just hate coming way out here to work for these white people?" To her regret, my wife replied that she didn't work in Chevy Chase; she lived there—end of conversation. A few blocks later, the lady made an excuse for not going to the Chevy Chase Circle and said my wife would have to get out.

Both the white man who propositioned me and the black lady who picked up my wife are probably not racists. Both were playing correct odds, namely, that if you saw a black in Chevy Chase at that time, he probably worked there. Race and physical appearances correlate nicely with other attributes. Both the white man and the black lady could have been a bit smarter about playing the correct odds, such as directly seeking additional information before their pronouncements.

In the wake of the "water buffalo" imbroglio at the University of Pennsylvania, black students complained about another form of racism: They are more frequently asked to show ID cards when entering dormitories than white students.

In Washington, D.C., there's a similar phenomenon. Taxi drivers, including black drivers, frequently pass up prospective black male customers, particularly at night. Might we accuse taxi drivers of racism? We can't be sure in either their case or that of dormitory guards at the University of Pennsylvania.

Whether we like it or not, race and crime are highly correlated. And, more important for dorm guards and taxi drivers, violent criminal acts are highly correlated to race. Black people know this, as do white people. Under certain circumstances, taking extra security precautions with a black person reduces the risk of being a crime victim.

By no stretch of the imagination is this fair to honest, law-abiding black people; it's insulting. But who creates the stereotype that imposes this unfair burden? It's not white people. Some white people don't like Japanese and Chinese, but they haven't been able to pin them with the criminal stereotype. Those who create the hurtful burden of the criminal stereotype for law-abiding black people are the tiny percentage of the black population who are thugs and hoodlums and commit a disproportionate percent of violent crime.

We must be more intelligent about race in order to solve racial problems. A good beginning is to recognize what is racism and what is not.

Sexual Harassment

June 14, 1993

According to anti–sexual harassment advocates, one is guilty of harassment simply by eye-to-eye or eye-to-bust contact. Being black, I'm sensitive to that risk. It wasn't long ago that a black man, gazing at a white woman, could be lynched for "reckless eyeballing" and "desiring to want." But here's the question: Shouldn't at least some women face charges of entrapment, or contributory negligence, for deliberately dressing so as to incite weak men into eye-to–gluteus maximus contact?

Then there are regulations against unwanted sexual advances in the workplace. Here's the problem: Unless you're a mind reader, how do you know when an advance is unwanted unless you advance? It's a problem known to economists as *asymmetric information*: one party has better information than the other. A woman may or may not want the advance, but the guy just doesn't get it. Keep in mind that the workplace is a valuable male/female meeting place, leading to acquaintance, romance, and very often marriage. But the asymmetric information problem can get you in trouble. Maybe women should be required to have a sexual harassment consent form in their personnel files that reads I consent to the following checked-off forms of behavior—eye-to-eye contact, eye-to-bust contact, salutatory greetings, heavy breathing on neck, ears, and other body parts, hands on shoulder, torso, gluteus maximus, and other. Given President Clinton's push to open the military to homosexuals, we might have the same form in the personnel folders of our fighting men. Male employees and soldiers would then have no flimsy excuses for making unwanted advances and could be summarily fired or discharged.

Of course, the tendency to sexually harass may be seen as a handicap, like alcohol and drug addiction. Thus, the Americans with Disabilities Act would come into play, and there'd have to be sexual harassment treatment programs. You may be interested in a treatment program I experienced. Forty-some years ago, as a student at Philadelphia's Stoddart-Fleisher Junior High School, I improperly touched a girl. It was on the fire-escape stairs. She turned around and kicked me down the stairs to the next landing, where I lay injured; then she proceeded to stomp on my stomach and chest. The pain was bad enough, but the years of ridicule and teasing that following were worse. But I was cured.

The Anita Hill fiasco proved that you can't prove a negative. In other words, if a woman falsely accuses me of blowing in her ear, how can I prove I didn't? Therefore, men must take defensive steps against the risk of sexual harassment accusations, particularly those in high-risk jobs. My heart goes out to patrolmen partnered with women. If she falsely accuses him of sexual harassment, what defense does he have? They were alone in the car. Police departments could install video cameras in cars. With advances in voice recognition technology, the camera could start recording as soon as a sex-based word is spoken. If I know guys, they can be slick. I imagine code phrases might emerge like, "You want to see my chemistry set?" or "How's the weather?" Departments might fight these blatantly evasive tactics by hiring referee/chaperon patrol officers to ride along, but what sex should the referee/ chaperon be? For right now, a policeman who cares about his job and reputation should refuse to be partnered with a woman.

Working in a highly charged sexual harassment environment, I'm creating a new modus operandi. If a female student or colleague asks to meet in private, I plan to have my secretary listen in, videotape, and transcribe the meeting. I'm also thinking about requiring females to sign affidavits attesting that no sexual harassment took place.

Disregarded Civil Liberties

SEPTEMBER 22, 1993

Monique Landers is a black fifteen-year-old high school student in Wichita, Kansas. With assistance from the National Foundation for Teaching Entrepreneurship (NFTE), she started A Touch of Class, a small business that washes and braids hair. With family members and friends as customers, she was able to earn about $100 in profits a month. She was so successful that she was called to New York to be honored as one of five outstanding high school entrepreneurs.

That's just one story about NFTE's successful program aimed at ghetto youth. Founded by Steve Mariotti and now in ten cities, NFTE teaches youths how to develop a business plan and market a product or service. Under its auspices, businesses started by at-risk youngsters include stereo component installers, desktop publishing, magicians, and baby-sitters. The kids are excited, energetic, enthusiastic, and learning practical lessons. I know. Earlier this year, I addressed what must have been three hundred proud students, parents, and teachers in NFTE's Wichita program.

You'd think everybody would say, "Great show, Steve Mariotti; somebody needs to be on the ground helping impoverished youth find a better way. Let's find out how to produce some more Monique Landers!" Think again. When the Kansas State Cosmetology Board heard about Monique's award, they sent a letter warning her that it was illegal for her to touch hair for profit without a license and that if she did not immediately cease her practice, she would be subject to "a fine or imprisonment in the county jail or both." Nancy Shobe, the board's director, says Monique should take a yearlong cosmetology program at a certified school to become licensed. First, there are not that many cosmetology schools that teach hair braiding. Second, tuition ranges from $2,500 to $5,500 for a nine-month course, plus the minimum age is seventeen.

Because braiding hair involves no use of chemicals, there is no public health issue. The customer's hair is washed, and the braider spends anywhere from two to eight hours weaving intricate patterns. The real issue is monopoly. According to a story in the *Wichita Eagle*, more than one hundred licensed cosmetologists complained to the Kansas board about Monique's lack of a license. Which do you think was the greater concern to those cosmetologists: the welfare of Monique's customers or the loss of business to Monique? If you guessed the latter, go to the head of the class.

Monique's experience is simply the tip of the ugly occupational licensing iceberg that cuts off the bottom rungs of the economic ladder. It's cruel that we sanction these collusive laws. Would we be more satisfied if Monique were having babies, getting welfare, and doing drugs? If she were, you can bet the authorities would not be nearly as relentless in their pursuit of "corrective" action.

In countless ways, poor people who are motivated are denied routes out of poverty available in the past. Instead of opportunity, they are given welfare. And it's not just enterprising kids. Houston, Texas, stopped a former taxicab driver from providing jitney services. New York and other cities periodically harass street vendors. More and more states legislate against private, unlicensed, small-scale day care services. Civil rights organizations and black politicians are silent and often support denial of opportunity. But they beg for handouts.

Monique's plight highlights the importance of the Washington-based Institute for Justice. The District of Columbia's licensing board tried to run Cornrows & Company, another braider, out of business. The institute represented its owner, Taalib-Din Abdul Aqdah, and won. Wouldn't it be great if civil rights organizations focused attention on economic liberties instead of constantly begging?

Update on the Sex Front

August 18, 1993

We all remember sobbing Lieutenant Paula Coughlin, who told ABC's Peter Jennings and us about her sexual abuse at the navy's 1991 Tailhook convention. She reported that she and other female navy officers had to walk a gauntlet while being pinched and fondled by navy male officers.

But there's another part of this story that Peter Jennings and the rest of the profeminist media won't tell. As a result of the incident, Liutenant Rolando Diaz, a navy E2 pilot, has been charged with "conduct unbecoming an officer." Why? Because he was shaving female navy officers' legs in his unit's hospitality suite during the Tailhook convention. But because charging him and not the female officers was tagged as an unfair double standard, the navy's now relying on "willful disobedience" to get Diaz.

"What's the willful disobedience?" you ask. Diaz's superior commander ordered him not to shave female navy officers' legs above the midthigh region. According to the navy deputy inspector general's report of the incident to the Department of Defense, a shaving booth was set up in the hospitality suite in full view of the pool patio. The booth consisted of a chair and a stool for two male officers. Leg shavings, which included the use of hot towels and baby oil, lasted 30 to 45 minutes, culminating in a "quality test," in which the female officers' legs were licked to check for stubble. The inspector general's report said that, in some cases, "Women's pubic areas were shaved as well in what was referred to as a 'bikini shave.'" The inspector general also reported coed "belly shots"—get ready—where alcoholic beverages are drunk from another's navel.

According to the inspector general, none of the women who had their legs shaved, including Lieutenant Paula Coughlin, complained of having been coerced. It was all part of the fun and games that were traditional at the navy's Tailhook convention. It's similar to the relatively harmless college postadolescent nonsense. But in an era of political correctness, where people search for victim status in pursuit of hidden agendas, Tailhook activities are a no-no.

Forget about Tailhook; think about fall. In the August 1993 edition of *Commentary*, Dana Mack says that the National Guidelines for Comprehensive Sexuality Education advises that children as young as five be taught that "it feels good to touch parts of the body," that "some men and women are homosexual, which means that they will be attracted to . . . someone of the same gender," and that "the man puts his penis in the woman's vagina, and that really feels good for both of them." At some schools, students are taught "how to stimulate their partner's erogenous zones, how to initiate casual sex, and how to keep it safe from pregnancy and disease." Mack says teachers have even asked boys, "How would you react if a boy asked you out?"

For the most part, sex education classes are part of the liberal agenda to undermine traditional family values and family authority. With Clinton appointees who have mind-sets like Joycelyn Elders, our new surgeon general, we can expect to see more undermining of family values and authority. Parents are not helpless in the face of this assault. They should get off their duff, read their children's books, demand to see teacher lesson plans, and sit in on classes. They should also be alert to behavioral changes in their children. Because most parents aren't like Williams—6 feet, 6 inches tall, 220 pounds, karate black belt, not to mention having a family full of hoodlums—they should organize a school boycott if they detect sex brainwashing.

No Civil Rights Problem

SEPTEMBER 8, 1993

This year's civil rights march on Washington proves that civil rights organizations just don't get it. The fact is, the civil rights struggle is over and it's won. At one time, black Americans' constitutional guarantees weren't protected. Now they are. Although every iota of racial discrimination hasn't disappeared, discrimination is nowhere near the barrier it once was.

The triumph of the civil rights struggle doesn't mean there aren't serious major problems. What it does mean is that they are not civil rights problems and hence will not be solved through a civil rights agenda. Let's look at it.

The illegitimacy rate among blacks is 65 percent. In some cities, we're talking 80 percent. Girls as young as nine years old are becoming mothers. Nearly 60 percent of black children live in female-headed households. In some cities, the black high school dropout rate exceeds 50 percent. Often those who manage to graduate have worthless, fraudulent diplomas. Rampant crime has made many black communities economic wastelands. Often residents must take precautions unheard of elsewhere—like meals served on the floor so as not to be hit by stray bullets.

These are all devastating problems, but they are not civil rights problems. Solutions will prove elusive if they're viewed as such. Indeed, if all white people became morally rejuvenated tomorrow, it would mean absolutely nothing for blacks who live under the pathological conditions seen in many inner cities. Plus, more money for welfare, poverty, and education programs holds little promise. After all, since 1965, at least $3.5 trillion dollars has been spent in the name of eliminating poverty.

That's the bad news. The good news is that solutions rest mostly in the hands of black people. What's needed is a "can do" vision and a rejection of the advice of policy makers, politicians, and experts. Blacks are increasingly taking the initiative of starting independent schools as an alternative to violent and fraudulent government schools. Black Wisconsin state legislator Polly Williams is leading the movement for school choice as a means to provide educational alternatives.

In Detroit and Camden, New Jersey, thugs have established a Halloween tradition of arson. Unable to count on police protection, last year residents patrolled the streets and arson was minimized.

Just these two examples demonstrate that ordinary black people can develop resources to address their problems. They don't need parasitic poverty pimps parachuting in bankrupt, half-baked, debilitating agendas from Washington, state capitols, and city halls.

Progress demands that inner-city residents take back their neighborhoods. When I say take back, I mean citizens should establish foot patrols, armed if necessary. "Williams," you say, "are you suggesting vigilantism?" Yes, I am, unless you're prepared to say what else people should do when authorities won't provide protection.

Government schools allow violent and disruptive pupils to make education impossible. Blacks who care about academic excellence should demand expulsion of these students. Should schools ignore this demand, black community organizations might consider physically denying disruptive students entry onto the school premises.

The state of affairs is desperate for about a third of the black population. There is no evidence that their problems will be solved by more promises and government programs. Something else must be tried immediately. If not, a large percentage of blacks will be utterly useless in the high-tech world of the twentieth century.

Going Wrong, Going Mad

NOVEMBER 3, 1993

If you're like me, listening to race experts, black politicians, and civil rights leaders, you'd think they've gone mad. They come just short of saying that white people meet every night to design ways to victimize black people. Blacks score lower on the SAT college entrance exam because whites design the test that way. Supermarket owners don't like black people's money so they leave black neighborhoods. Courts and police are racist because blacks are incarcerated in numbers that far exceed our numbers in the population. Racism is the root cause of every black problem. White people have God-like powers. They make black males produce babies and desert them. Whites make blacks murder each other. They make blacks rob, steal, and pillage black neighborhoods.

These devil-made-me-do-it excuses are really a part of a tragic attempt to conceal the failure and absolute bankruptcy of past promises and programs. Take schooling: Since the 1960s, race experts have been telling us that what's needed to improve black education is more innovative programs, more black role models, and, of course, more money. Now, in 1993, in cities like Washington, D.C.—which has a black superintendent of schools and a large number of black administrators, principals, and teachers to serve as role models and which spends $7,550 per pupil—black educational results are the pits. If you were an advocate of all this, in the name of promoting black education, what do you do? Would you say, "I was a fool"? Or do you chalk the failure up to racism, not enough money, and the "last twelve years." When miseducated black kids go off to college deceived into thinking they had a good high school education and suffer academic difficulties and flunk out, what do they and the affirmative action lady do? Admit that many black students can't meet college standards because of fraudulent precollege preparation or attack college standards as racist and call for dumbing down in pursuit of the bogus minutiae of diversity and multiculturalism?

Part of the solution of the educational problem is to recognize that, even if you're whiter than white, if your parents don't make you go to bed on time, do your homework, and mind the teacher, a job test or college admission test is going to look like a vicious attack on you.

Blacks spend enough money each year to make us, if we were a nation, the fourteenth richest. I guarantee you that white supermarket owners and white bankers love dollars coming from black people. The reason they leave, or choose not to enter, some black neighborhoods has much more to do with the costs of crime than with racism. Instead of serious efforts to reduce crime, people are talking about "enterprise zones" with subsidies and other payoffs to stimulate economic activity in decayed black neighborhoods. How much of a tax write-off is necessary to get the average businessman to put up with drive-by shootings and other terrors that are the daily fare in many black communities?

Blacks must reject the race hustler's pablum and go back to square one. A square-one agenda includes a demand for accountability, responsibility, high standards, and an individual sense of proprietorship when it comes down to schools, businesses, and neighborhoods. To the lawless, troublemakers, and assorted misfits, we must say, "I don't know what your problem is, and I hope you get better, but you're not going to mess it up for everybody else." We can't look to white people and Washington for the solution; it's a black thing.

Destructive Liberal Pandering

DECEMBER 8, 1993

Sitting in Rush Limbaugh's Attila the Hun chair for a day last September, I gave a present to America's white liberals: I granted them full pardon and general amnesty for both their own grievances and those of their forebears against my people. The reason for that magnanimous gesture was to reduce white guilt in the hopes that white liberals would stop acting like fools—at least on matters of race.

I shall occupy the Attila the Hun chair again the week after Christmas. There's going to be an entire hour devoted to guilt-reduction therapy for white liberals. Hopefully, President Clinton will agree to be my telephone guest as my first guilt anxiety/relief patient. You say, "Williams, why Clinton?"

Clinton was selected because of an excellent *Washington Post* (11/20/93) article by John Ray, a black member of the Council of the District of Columbia. It covered Clinton's speech at the Memphis church where Martin Luther King delivered his last address. Invoking the name of Dr. King many times, Clinton said, "The freedom to die before you're a teen-ager is not what Martin Luther King lived and died for." As for gang violence, Clinton said, "We will take away their guns and give them books," and "We will take away their despair and give them hope." Then Clinton called for a church, business, and government partnership to revive family values in black youth in order to "honor the life and work of Dr. King."

Councilman John Ray pointed out that it is demeaning to insult the "legacy of the civil rights movement by burdening it with the responsibility for the conduct of hoodlums who have no knowledge of, interest in, the struggle for civil rights." Ray says we are witnessing the kind of hard-core gangsterism that this country has not experienced since the days of Al Capone. But here's the kicker. John Ray pointed out that "when Al Capone terrorized the Midwest with mob violence, we didn't send for preachers to counsel him and his goons. We sent in squads of federal, state and local lawmen to kick butt and take names. We went to war against the mob and stopped the violence."

That is not a profound idea; it's just plain common sense. I'm positive Clinton and other white liberals have the brains to come to the identical conclusion about how to stop the wanton slaughter in many black neighborhoods. It's a backbone problem. It's a guilt-induced fear of possibly being called a racist—hence, my therapy session. But I could be all wrong about guilt as a motivator. There is a long-standing tradition whereby if a liberal has an idea that has never worked nowhere nohow, he'll try it out on black people. Clinton's idea about a church, business, and government partnership to reduce gang violence might be yet another one of those experiments on black people. I don't recall Elliot Ness asking for a church, business, and government partnership to deal with the Chicago mobs.

John Ray says, "We can no longer shield, excuse or rationalize outrageous criminal behavior that treats human life as if it were worthless." Councilman Ray's suggestion to Clinton: "Mr. President, the thugs who are plying their deadly trade on America's streets don't deserve to be mentioned in the same breath as Dr. King. They deserve to be led to a jail cell, not to the promised land." Guilt-ridden white liberals, with their pseudosophistication in psychobabble and sociobabble probably label John Ray's suggestion "blaming the victim."

White liberals might not need my guilt therapy for a cure. They might just as easily be permanently cured by the requirement that they spend a year or two living in a high-crime inner-city neighborhood.

Racism Is Racism

DECEMBER 15, 1993

Colin A. Ferguson's rampage, killing five New York commuter passengers and wounding twenty others, proves whites don't have a monopoly on racism. If civil rights organizations, black politicians, and ministers are to keep whatever modicum of rapidly diminishing creditability they still have, they must roundly condemn both Ferguson's racist behavior and his apologists. So far, I have not heard civil rights organizations' calling a press conference to do that. You can bet the rent money that, had a white person committed similar mayhem in Harlem, it would be show time for the likes of Al Sharpton, Jesse Jackson, and Benjamin Chavis.

The liberal news media couldn't hide this act of racism like they've hidden other acts of barbaric black racism. For instance, in July 1989, Danny Gilmore was driving his pickup truck through a black neighborhood in Cleveland. He had a minor accident with a moped rider and was set on and beaten by a group of roughly forty blacks. When he collapsed on the street, one of them drove Gilmore's truck over him, fatally crushing his skull, to the cheers of the mob. In January 1991, Robert Herbert and three other blacks agreed that they would kill the first white person they saw. Mark Belmore, a white student at Northeastern University, had the bad luck. He was stabbed to death. In February 1991, Christopher Peterson was arrested for murdering seven white people with a shotgun. He explained his actions by saying "he had a deep-rooted hatred for white people."

According to Department of Justice statistics, when whites commit violent crimes, blacks are their victims 2.4 percent of the time; however, blacks choose white victims more than 50 percent of the time. Blacks murder whites twice as often as whites murder blacks. Black-on-white gang robberies are fifty-two times greater than white on black. Black men rape white women thirty times more than white men rape black women.

Blacks are the primary victims of violent crime. Pick up a newspaper in cities like New York, Philadelphia, Detroit, and Los Angeles. You won't see a day pass without one black being murdered—and that's on a good day. But the interracial aspect of crime is especially socially devastating. It not only destroys racial goodwill, but it contributes to a rising pile of racial kindling awaiting a racial arsonist to set it ablaze.

There's a world of evidence that multiethnic societies are inherently unstable. We need only to witness the recent history of Bosnia, Nigeria, Sri Lanka, Lebanon, and others to see that. We risk similar conflict unless we quickly summon the courage to speak openly and honestly about our racial problems. We must condemn a president and other politicians who see the Ferguson carnage as a gun-control problem. When the Ku Klux Klan was murdering blacks, I don't recall our treating it as a gun-and-rope problem. We rightly saw it as racism. Those grossly ignorant academics, media people, and politicians who announce that blacks cannot be racists because they have no power must be condemned. All racial double standards must be eliminated immediately.

The primary burden for racial openness and honesty lies with blacks. But whites bear a major burden as well. As Senator Bill Bradley (D-N.J.) said in a 1991 letter to President Bush, "We will never come to grips with the problems of our cities . . . until a white person can talk about the epidemic of minority illegitimacy, drug addiction and homicide without being called a racist."

Language and Race

JANUARY 14, 1994

Philosopher Jeremy Bentham said, "Error is never so difficult to be destroyed as when it has roots in language." To see his point, let's ask, Are the water fountains at Amtrak's Washington train station, once racially segregated, now desegregated? The average person would answer yes. What would be his test? He'd watch to see whether a black, wanting a drink, has unimpaired access.

Now ask, Are the nation's schools, many of which were segregated, now desegregated? Honest people, observing identical phenomena, wouldn't agree. Many would say schools are desegregated, but many more, including academics like Harvard professor Gary Orfield, who recently reported schools are even more segregated than they were in the past, would say schools are still segregated.

Here's the problem. The definition of desegregation, and its test, shifts when we go from water fountains to schools. In the case of water fountains, the test is whether a black can take a drink if he's at the station. For many, the test for school desegregation is whether blacks actually attend some school according to their numbers in the population. No one would apply the same definition of desegregation to water fountains. In other words, no one would conclude that, because blacks are 70 percent of the population of Washington and only 15 percent of the water fountain users at the train station are black, the fountains are segregated. Because a sensible definition is used, there's no call to bus blacks from the water fountains in Anacostia, a predominantly black neighborhood, to those at the train station in the name of racial equality.

If the same definition of desegregation were applied to schools, we'd find that schools have been desegregated, the sensible test being whether a black parent residing in a particular neighborhood has the right to send her child to the same public school as her next-door neighbor.

What people really mean when they say schools are segregated is that they don't find the racial mix at some schools pleasing. But so what. If that's the vision of fairness and equality, ice hockey games are also "unpleasing" in terms of the racial composition of the audience and players, as are Pavarotti concerts, violin recitals, and nature walks through the Grand Canyon. In these and many other instances, blacks are grossly underrepresented in terms of their percentages in society.

"But, Williams," you say, "schools are rotten in many black neighborhoods; what are we going to do?" The answer's the same as if you said the fountains were broken in black neighborhoods. We fix them. "Come on, Williams," you reply, "even the Supreme Court said separate but equal education is inherently unequal!" Don't misunderstand me. I don't call for separate education, but there is no evidence whatsoever that academic excellence cannot occur at racially homogeneous schools. In fact, it happens every day at black private schools like Chicago's Westside Preparatory, Philadelphia's Ivy Leaf, Los Angeles's Marcus Garvey, and a few public schools with strong principals who've ignored edicts of the central authorities.

The reason math is easy is because it contains rigorous definitions. For example, zero is defined as any number when added to or subtracted from another number does not change the value of that number. Maybe social science definitions can't be as rigorous, but let's try. It will spare us some grief.

Civil Rights Struggle Won

MARCH 28, 1994

Black history has been a struggle for basic civil rights. Although problems remain, the fact is that the civil rights struggle is over and it's won. If you need supporting evidence, look at the degeneration of our flagship civil rights organization—the National Association for the Advancement of Colored People (NAACP). Its agenda today would have been inconceivable during the 1950s and 1960s. A few years ago, it worried about whether Arizona made Martin Luther King's birthday an official holiday. It frets about the Confederate flag flying over state buildings in Alabama and Georgia. Last year, it nominated rap singer Tupac Shakur for its Image Award. Tupac had been indicted for shooting two Atlanta policemen, not to mention being charged with holding down a New York woman while his buddies raped her. As if decadence had no downside, Benjamin Chavis, the NAACP's new director, equated Los Angeles hoodlum Rodney King to Martin Luther King at the "Gang Summit." Jesse Jackson praised the assembled gang members as "the vanguard of the new civil rights movement."

Black politicians, self-appointed "leaders," and the NAACP try to convince blacks there's racism behind every problem. When they can't identify a flesh-and-bones racist, it's "institutional" racism. Yesteryear, it was easy to be a racist. All you needed was a cross, a white suit, and a vocabulary. Today, you can be a racist by calling for limited government, educational vouchers, and longer jail sentences. The surest way to be a modern racist is to demand equal treatment by race in college admissions, jobs, and housing.

Don't get me wrong—the NAACP played a vital role in winning constitutional guarantees for black Americans. Moreover, if civil rights was still a problem, you can bet that able blacks would wrest the organization's leadership from today's dimwits. In its death throes, the NAACP leaders have become little more than useful idiots for homosexuals and radical feminists whose agenda in no way benefits those for whom the NAACP speaks, as it hustles and extorts money from guilt-ridden, weak-kneed corporate CEOs.

Right now, the NAACP is being used by homosexuals and radical feminists to intimidate the Florida Citrus Commission into canceling advertisements on the "Rush Limbaugh Show." They see Limbaugh as a racist, homophobe, and sexist simply because he espouses limited government, jailing criminals, two-parent families, high educational standards, and, worst of all, traditional values shared by most Americans. So far, the Florida Citrus Commission has hung tough and resisted pressures from spokesmen for Florida governor Lawton Chiles and feminist/homosexual activists.

Then, how about this? The Washington-based Institute for Justice is waging battle in the courts and the Colorado legislature on behalf of would-be black taxi owners. They want to break the state's restrictive, monopolistic taxicab regulations. Guess what? The local branch of the NAACP supports the effort, but the national office refuses to help. The why is easy. The Teamsters Union is for the monopoly. The NAACP and most black politicians do the bidding of unions even though the union agenda is, and has always been, against the economic interests of blacks. But the union payback is to cast a few peanuts to black politicians and give them lobby assistance for handouts.

The bottom line: If white people were to become morally rejuvenated tomorrow, it would do nothing for the problems plaguing a large segment of the black community. Illegitimacy, family breakdown, crime, and fraudulent education are devastating problems, but they are not civil rights problems. They won't be solved by civil rights strategy and mentality.

Liberals Created Black Racism

JUNE 22, 1994

People are shocked, dismayed, and perplexed over a significant portion of the black community's seeming endorsement or silence over the plainly racist and anti-Semitic diatribes of Nation of Islam minister Louis Farrakhan and his disciple Khalid Muhammad.

Stripped of racism, anti-Semitism, and nationalism, Minister Farrakhan's message to blacks is get off welfare and get a job, stop depending on white people and be independent, stop using drugs, stop criminal preying on the black community, stop having babies out of wedlock, take responsibility for yourself, show respect for black women, and put some prayer into your lives.

Ironically, that message contains much of the argument that conservative blacks have been making for several decades. There's been warning after warning against the leftist deliverance of poor blacks into the debilitating clutches of the welfare state and its spiritual and moral destruction.

Conservative blacks have warned against abandoning traditional values and substituting those values with alternative lifestyles. However, conservative criticism of the half-baked schemes of the 1960s and 1970s was greeted with scorn and belittlement by establishment blacks, black politicians, civil rights leaders, and white liberals. With media complicity, blacks who preached the nonracist elements of the Farrakhan message were condemned as "selling out," "blaming the victim," and "giving aid and comfort to America's racists." It was easy to dismiss the messenger but not the message or its reality.

Liberal ideas have been especially devastating to the black underclass. Because "original causes" could not be eliminated, liberals have accepted a level of criminal activity and property destruction that has turned many black neighborhoods into economic wastelands. Liberals have used a bad home environment as an excuse to permit hostile, disruptive kids to stay in school and make education impossible for everybody else. Slavery and racism have been used as an excuse for out-of-wedlock births, and welfare has been promoted as a substitute for fathers.

Conservatives have always argued this was nonsense. Farrakhan's successful nationalistic appeal results from black and white liberals' success in snuffing out civil criticism and discourse. Suppression of alternative ideas created the vacuum so ably filled by Farrakhan and his disciples. From what I know of Nation of Islam philosophy, behavior justified by those excuses is not tolerated and surely is not encouraged.

It's easy for Minister Farrakhan and others to indict racism for today's problems. After all, forty years after *Brown vs. Board of Education*, black education is in shambles and, in many cases, worse than it was in 1954. The nation has allocated massive resources to fight discrimination and create affirmative action programs. But for many blacks, college and a decent job are an unrealizable dream. Predominantly black-populated cities face fiscal chaos, social disarray, and an exodus (black and white) of their most productive people. The gross failure of the programs of the 1960s and 1970s to deliver on their promises helps make charges of "institutional racism" and "subtle racism" seem plausible. For many people, what else can explain the failure of good intentions and costly social programs to deliver on the promises?

Had conservative critics not been silenced and liberal ideas not gone unchallenged, not only wouldn't we see today's level of black racism, there would be far less poverty and despair. In the process of using poor black people to further their ideological, income, and political agenda, liberals have produced the conditions for Minister Louis Farrakhan's popularity. A conservative challenge to liberal lunacy is long overdue, too bad that it's cloaked in racism, anti-Semitism, and nationalism.

Our Liberal Enemies

OCTOBER 3, 1994

Last week, in Houston, Texas, I attended the National Minority Politics Conference, an organization founded by Gwen Daye-Richardson. Assembled were about five hundred blacks and a few whites, mostly from the Houston area. Some participants came from as far away as Los Angeles. It was a moderate-to-conservative group, not Williams-type radicals. The discussion focused on what was necessary to reverse the social pathology so prevalent in most black inner-city neighborhoods.

There wasn't the lingua franca of the conventional civil rights crowd, where racism is the cause of everything and more government spending is the cure. The conferees talked mostly about what black people could do for themselves. There must be a rejection of government undermining family values. We must stop glamorizing destructive behavior that leads to illegitimacy. Education won't be improved until we rid schools of thugs. We need strong law enforcement to lower the devastating crime rate.

Ezola Foster, president of Americans for Family Values, Starr Parker, president of the Los Angeles–based Coalition on Urban Affairs, Robert Woodson, director of the National Center for Neighborhood Enterprises, and Jesse Peterson, founder of Brotherhood Organization of a New Destiny, were among the many speakers the traditional civil rights establishment thinks of as "Uncle Toms." But history is going to tell a different story, and it's going to be the liberal hustlers and poverty pimps who are revealed as the true sellouts.

You say, "That's some pretty heavy language, Williams; back it up!" The most serious damage done to blacks is the result of stupid liberal ideas that haven't worked noplace nohow. The liberals' idea of an anticrime strategy is to search for original causes and organize midnight basketball games. In the meantime, law-abiding black people live in fear for their property and lives. Crime has made doing business so costly that businesses flee black neighborhoods. Liberals respond by getting the Justice Department to go after banks who choose not to locate branches or make loans in such an unattractive economic environment. Liberals ask us to believe white bankers don't like dollars and profits coming from black hands.

The liberal "solution" for teenage pregnancy is sex education (read attacking traditional values), condom distribution, and birth control. For them, teaching chastity is a religious right-wing conspiracy. You can evaluate the success of those liberal ideas. Teen pregnancy was not a problem before there were programs liberals say are necessary.

The liberal solution to what's no less than educational fraud delivered by government schools is always to call for more money and with that money create education programs that would only win the confidence of lunatics and intellectuals. They call for Afrocentrism so black kids will have greater self-esteem, leading to higher academic achievement. For them, the reason white kids score higher is because white kids get up in the morning, look into the mirror, and ponder, "Homer wrote *The Iliad* and *The Odyssey*. Homer was white. Therefore, I am somebody."

In some cities, blacks have enacted curfew laws only to have liberals in the American Civil Liberties Union (ACLU) take them to court. In Baltimore and Detroit, blacks tried to start single-sex schools. Again, the ACLU, accompanied by the National Organization for Women gang, challenged them.

I have no doubt that blacks are about to become the staunchest conservative group in America, and the why is that liberalism has done to blacks what slavery, Jim Crowism, and the rankest racism combined could never have done.

GOVERNMENT

If we had to name the one institution that has been the enemy of humankind, it would be governments around the world, including our own. The essence of government is coercion, and by and large coercion is evil. A certain amount of government power and coercion is necessary for the preservation of liberty. Government needs to have the power to prevent those who would deny others the right to engage in peaceable, voluntary exchange, be the perpetrators foreign or domestic. Thus, one legitimate function of a federal government is to provide for national defense; state and local levels of government should provide police protection. Government must also have the power to adjudicate disputes among its citizens and enforce constitutional order.

Much of what federal, state, and local governments do today far exceeds constitutional authority and any reasonable definition of moral government. Our federal government is increasingly becoming destructive of the ends it was created to serve. Constitutional principles and rule of law are alien values in today's America. As Friedrich Hayek warned, "The important point is that all coercive action of government must be unambiguously determined by a permanent legal framework which enables the individual to plan with a degree of confidence and which reduces human uncertainty [and economic insecurity] as much as possible." We have made a mockery of the inscription carved into the wall at the U.S. Department of Justice, "Where the law ends tyranny begins." Federal and state agencies have used Nazi-style justice when people are declared to be criminals, not on the basis of their actions but on the consequences of their actions.

The most frequent column that I write has to do with how Con-

gress, acting at the behest of powerful interest groups, infringes one liberty of ours or another. I talk frequently, maybe preach, about how Congress, using its agents at the Internal Revenue Service, confiscates the rightful property of one American to give it to another to whom it does not belong and how Congress creates a special privilege for one American that comes at the expense of another.

The rule of thumb that I use for evaluating whether a particular act of government is moral or not is to ask, as does Frederic Bastiat, a French philosopher who wrote The Law, *"See if the law takes from some persons what belongs to them, and gives it to other persons to whom it does not belong. See if the law benefits one citizen at the expense of another by doing what the citizen himself cannot do without committing a crime." For example, can I interfere with your ingress or egress to your place of work and threaten you without being arrested? If I cannot, how is it that government protects union members doing so? Can I use intimidation, threats, and coercion to take your money to help a poor person, a farmer, or a failing S&L without going to jail? However, we allow, even ask and beg congressmen to do the same thing under the color of the law. Americans must ask whether an act clearly immoral and criminal when done privately becomes moral when done collectively and given legal sanction. The unambiguous answer will be that legality is a poor guide to morality. After all, slavery and apartheid were legal, as were the Nazi persecution of Jews and the Stalinist and Maoist purges. But the fact of being legal did not make them moral acts.*

The columns that follow address these and other issues about the increasingly immoral conduct of our government.

The Balanced Budget Hoax

JUNE 5, 1992

When history's biggest spenders, President Bush and the House and Senate cosponsors, come out in support of the proposed Balanced Budget Amendment to the U.S. Constitution, there must be some sinister, loathsome scheme afoot. We don't need a balanced budget as much as we need a limit on what Congress can take from us. Let's take a quick tour of government spending.

In 1787, federal spending was about $3 million a year, or about $1 a citizen. By 1910, the Feds spent a little more than $600 million, about $6.75 a person. By 1929, the Feds spent $3 billion a year, $29 a person. Today, the federal government spends more than $4 billion a day! That comes to more than $6,000 a year a person, or, controlling for inflation, a 9,000 percent increase in federal spending between 1929 and today. The colonists, who were paying about 67 cents a year in taxes, went to war with Great Britain, claiming, "Taxation without representation is tyranny." For my part, you can have taxation with representation; I'll take mine without.

The framers had a great distrust for Congress. We can see this distrust in the language of our Bill of Rights: shall not disparage, shall not infringe, and shall not be taken. Thomas Jefferson said, "And to preserve independence, we must not let our rulers load us with perpetual debt. We must make our election [choice] between economy and liberty, or profusion and servitude." You tell me, which combination have Americans chosen?

The proposed Balanced Budget Amendment requires that estimated federal expenditures not exceed estimated revenues, except in times of declared war or when Congress approves excess expenditures by a three-fifths vote. Aside from the amendment being a big-spender's paradise, I will tell you right now that the scoundrels in Congress have no intent of doing the right thing. "Hey, Williams," you say, "don't you have any faith in Congress?" Let's look at the record. Congress passed the Budget Control Act of 1974. Is the budget in control? In 1979, Congress passed the Balanced Budget Act, which made a balanced budget the law of the land. Remember the 1984 tax increases that were widely publicized and sold to Americans as a "down payment on the deficit"? How about the 1985 Gramm-Rudman-Hollings Emergency Deficit Reduction Act, which mandated a balanced budget by 1993? How about the tax increases of the 1990 budget deal to bring the 1992 deficit in at $168 billion, which instead stands at $400 billion? I don't know about you, but with a record like that, I conclude that the people in Congress and the White House are little more than liars, hustlers, and con artists.

There are no protections for our economic liberties in the proposed Balanced Budget Act. Look at it. Federal spending is now $1.5 trillion, while revenues are $1.1 trillion. Would we have more liberty if the federal budget were balanced at $2 trillion or $3 trillion or $4 trillion? If we go for the balanced budget rope-a-dope, we will have given Congress a perfect excuse to gouge us to death; it'll claim, "the Constitution requires it."

Some years ago, the Sacramento-based National Tax Limitation Committee, headed by Lewis K. Uhler, worked on a spending limitation amendment to the Constitution, which ultimately passed the Senate in 1982 but was sandbagged by the House. As described in Uhler's excellent, highly readable book *Setting Limits: Constitutional Control of Government,* the strongest version of the 1982 Balanced Budget/ Spending Limitation Amendment would have given Congress a bottom line, roughly 20 percent of the gross national product, plus any member of Congress would have standing before the Supreme Court to enforce compliance.

Test your member of Congress's sincerity, demand a spending limitation provision in the proposed Balanced Budget Act and watch him lie.

Manufactured Handicaps

FEBRUARY 3, 1993

Poor people have legitimate beefs but not those decried by liberals. Let's think it through. Suppose I were an owner of a large supermarket chain, and I wanted to forestall new competition, what might I do? The most successful strategy would be to raise costs to new entrants. I'd lobby at the state capitol and Washington or give support to groups pushing for stringent regulations mandating costly food-storage facilities, costly worker-safety provisions, and costly food-handling equipment. Without these regulations, you might need $800,000 to get into the market business; with them it costs another several hundred thousand dollars more. With this strategy, I come off as a civic-minded person "concerned" with public health, safety, and welfare and you're out on the street.

Now let's get down to cases. Sixty-two percent of poor households own at least one car. Acquiring a minivan is within reach. They could get into the taxicab or airport limousine business. However, the license for a single taxi costs as much as $140,000 in New York City and ranges between $15,000 and $85,000 elsewhere. Public utility commissions systematically legislate roadblocks to entry into airport limousine services. And who do you think pushes for these restrictions—customers and people who want to get in or those who are already in?

Say there's an old gasoline station, and you want to start an automated car-wash business. The previous owner had drained and concreted the old tanks, and there are no leaks. In addition to getting the capital for the car-washing equipment, Environmental Protection Agency regulations require that you spend anywhere between $35,000 and $50,000 digging up the old tanks and treating the land.

You might want to start a restaurant. In addition to other regulations that didn't apply to owners ten or twenty years ago, the Americans with Disabilities Act mandates that you build costly handicap facilities that may never be used. Established companies, which often support these and other costly measures like mandated health insurance and other bureaucratic regulations, retain staffs of lawyers and lobbyists, unlike the fledgling entrepreneur.

How about this one? Labor unions and some corporations push for laws mandating that U.S. companies who open factories in Mexico obey our costly safety and environmental laws. They push for higher wages for Mexican workers. My question to you is, Do you really think they care about the safety and pay of Mexican workers and the quality of the air they breathe? Or might a more satisfactory explanation be that they are trying to raise the cost to U.S. companies to locate in Mexico in an attempt to keep them here in order to have higher wages, product prices, and profits?

People are priced out of the labor market by the unions and the large, contractor-supported, racially motivated Davis-Bacon Act, which mandates superminimum wages in all federally funded or assisted construction. Even though black contractors and local black self-help groups have consistently come out against it, black congressmen, doing the bidding of unions, support the Davis-Bacon Act.

Black legislators support virtually every bit of legislation that raises the cost of business or job entry. It's not that black legislators are deliberately selling their people down the river or that they are stupid. They've made self-interested political alliances against the interests of their most disadvantaged constituency. It's what you might call government, business, and union cooperation. For their part in that cooperation, black politicians get welfare crumbs to distribute to their people.

SS American-Style

APRIL 28, 1993

President Clinton chose Easter Sunday to play a little politics by accusing Senator Robert Dole and his filibustering Republican colleagues of holding America's children hostage. A week later, the president had to call a press conference to take responsibility for his and Attorney General Janet Reno's decision that led to the deaths of twenty-four American children and sixty-four adults.

Because of previous outrages, twelve years ago, Representative John Dingell described the Treasury Department's Bureau of Alcohol, Tobacco and Firearms (BATF) as "jackbooted fascists." Little has changed since then. His son, John Dingell Jr., related in a *Wall Street Journal* article (3/15/93) similarities between our black-uniformed, "coal scuttle"–helmeted, machine pistol–toting BATF agents and Nazi SS agents who, fifty years earlier, similarly dressed and equipped, attacked the Jewish compound in Warsaw, Poland.

That's not the only similarity. Janet Reno gave suspicion of child abuse as partial justification for the government's actions. That's exactly what the Nazi news media told Germans about Jews—they were involved in sexual rituals involving children. Like the BATF, Nazi SS men said they were searching for illegal weapons, reported by paid informants, in the Warsaw ghetto. When SS agents stormed the ghetto, Warsaw Jews put up a fierce resistance, killing eleven of them and wounding many more. The SS had to call in armored military units for assistance. The BATF/FBI's armored units didn't use bullets and shells. They used O-chlorobenzalmalonnitrile, known as CS gas, banned for use in war by the Paris Chemical Weapons Convention.

The Clinton people owe us answers. From what I've learned, the

Branch Davidians, despite their constitutionally protected strange religious beliefs, were model citizens. They kept to themselves and harmed no one. Members were there voluntarily. David Koresh's lawyer says the children were well fed and cared for; there was no child abuse. Besides, when has child abuse come under the jurisdiction of either the BATF or the FBI?

One might argue that Koresh didn't heed the BATF warrant to search the premises. Just because a judge authorizes a search doesn't make the search right. If one has not committed a crime against someone, what business is it of the government how many and what type of guns a person possesses? The BATF/FBI allegation of stockpiling weapons is so much hogwash. Perhaps they should tell us what's the legal number of semiautomatic weapons. Even if five hundred weapons are found at the compound, that's not even eight to an adult.

Economist Paul Craig Roberts asks, in the *Washington Times* (4/22/93), if the two Los Angeles policemen are guilty of violating Rodney King's civil rights through excessive use of billy clubs, what kind of use-of-force judgment must we make against Clinton, Attorney General Reno, the BATF, and the FBI that led to the deaths of twenty-four children and sixty-four adults? Clinton said that Koresh and the Branch Davidians are responsible for what happened to them because they resisted the BATF and FBI. That's identical to the defense given by the four Los Angeles police officers who beat Rodney King—he could have ended the beating any time by submitting to authority.

There are other "cults." I bet Utah's Mormons have loads of guns. Will they be the next BATF/FBI victims? You really have to wonder what our country is coming to when people who go about their lives bothering no one, minding their business, and cherishing their privacy are subject to a vicious attack by their government while muggers, thieves, rapists, and murderers run rampant.

Secession

OCTOBER 20, 1993

Clinton's effort to forcibly impose socialized medicine on our nation has answered a question gnawing at me for quite some time. The question is, Have we reached a point where those of us who love liberty, private property rights, rule of law, and the Constitution given to us by our founding fathers should organize to make preparations to secede from the union?

Don't get me wrong. Clinton's plan for socialized medicine is just the latest straw in the heap of federal government assaults on liberty. The national debate over his plan, like so many other federal assaults on our liberties, focuses on whether it's a good plan or a bad plan. The totally ignored fundamental question is whether federalized medicine is authorized by the United States Constitution. My thorough reading of our Constitution found no authorization for Clinton's plan. For that matter, neither is there constitutional authority for up to two-thirds of federal government taxes and expenditures.

You say, "If you're right, Williams, how come none of our congressmen raise the issue?" The answer's easy. Most congressmen are charlatans who are either ignorant or contemptuous of our Constitution. In this atmosphere, the five or six congressmen who respect our Constitution fear being labeled as cranks and thereby risk losing credibility for raising constitutional questions. You say, "How about the U.S. Supreme Court?" It's the same atmosphere, with the exception of two or three justices who are similarly intimidated.

Again, don't get me wrong. I have nothing against socialism and socialists per se. My only problem is that they want to use the brutal force of government to force me and others who simply want to be left alone to be a part of their schemes. I respect liberty so much that I am willing to grant to others the right to live their lives as they wish and ask that they permit the same to others. However, the president, Congress, and the court view that vision, variously described as "natural law" or "unalienable rights," with contempt, as we witnessed during the Clarence Thomas hearings.

The only peaceful resolution is that of secession. Not having given much thought to an actual plan of secession, and not having the expertise to do so in the first place, I'd be willing to cede all the territory except the thirteen original states and Texas to America's socialists. "Hey, Williams," you say, "the last time secession was tried, we had a pretty bloody war." You're right, but let's hope that we learned how costly it is to make people be a part of something they don't want to be. After all, the right to part company is the most effective human safety valve, no matter whether it's divorce, quitting a job, or secession. If there's a ban on parting company, somebody's likely to be treated like a dog. Indeed, because states are seen as not having the right of secession, plus de facto repeal of the Tenth Amendment, the federal government is able to ride roughshod over liberty-loving people, thus trashing Article IV of the constitutional mandate "The United States shall guarantee to every State in the Union a Republican Form of government."

I would hope that secession wouldn't be bloody. And it wouldn't be if the nation's socialists adopted the attitude of live and let live. But if they don't, liberty-loving people shouldn't roll over, play dead, and take socialists' abuses without imposing high costs in return.

Government Health Care

DECEMBER 8, 1993

There's a real health tragedy unfolding that's guaranteed to become more tragic if Congress adopts any feature of the Clinton health proposal. A taste of this tragedy is found in the summer 1993 issue of *Policy Review* in a story, really a plea, by Lois Copeland, M.D.

The government imposes price ceilings on Medicare reimbursements that will become nationwide if Clinton has his way. Dr. Copeland charges non-Medicare patients $60 for an office visit. The maximum Medicare reimbursement is $36.81. Her initial hospitalization fee for non-Medicare is $275 vs. $122.71 under Medicare, and an EKG is $50 vs. $32.22. Surgeons in her town of Bergen, New Jersey, get hit even worse. Surgical fees for carpal tunnel release, a common wrist procedure, run from $1,200 to $2,000, but the maximum Medicare reimbursement is $300.

The government freeze on Medicare reimbursements doesn't keep down other costs such as malpractice premiums, mountains of government paperwork requirements, medical equipment, and rising salaries of office staff. Dr. Copeland says she could have solved her dilemma, as many other doctors do, by refusing additional Medicare patients, by refusing them timely appointments, or by telling her existing Medicare patients to find other doctors. But she says that a number of her older patients are her friends. Then she says, "How can I refuse to treat a sick patient?"

If it costs Dr. Copeland $50 to do an EKG, what's wrong with a Medicare patient saying, "I don't want you to be ripped off, so let Medicare reimburse you the $32.22, and I'll write you a check for $17.78"? That's fine, but in Canada's socialized medical system and ours under the Clinton plan, it's against the law. Dr. Copeland makes up for the Medicare shortfall, as do other doctors, by charging younger patients higher fees. She points out that this is perverse because her younger patients are far less wealthy than her Medicare patients, who are likely to own their homes and have fewer debts.

Dr. Copeland has another alternative that she doesn't mention. She could try billing Medicare for services not rendered or order unnecessary tests to make up for the Medicare shortfall. No doubt some doctors have opted for that solution. But Dr. Copeland is far too principled. Instead, she organized some of her Medicare patients to join her in a lawsuit, assisted by the American Health Legal Foundation and Freedom of Choice Fund, that challenged Medicare's prohibition against private contracts. Her case became known as *Stewart v. Sullivan.* Oral arguments were heard in September 1992 in the federal court in Newark, New Jersey. Judge Nicholas Politan held that Louis Sullivan, President Bush's secretary of health and human services, had not issued a clear statement against private contracting and, even if he had, such a policy would constitute an "injury in fact," thus giving Dr. Copeland and her patients standing to sue.

Health care practitioners should make themselves knowledgeable of the *Stewart v. Sullivan* decision. But, even more important, doctors should rebel against the political cowardice demonstrated by the American Medical Association, which has rolled over in the face of a proposal by President Clinton that will cripple the world's best medical care system. All of us might read Aesop's fable about a dog and his bone. A dog crosses a bridge carrying a bone. He looks into the river and sees its reflection. The bone in the river looks bigger, and he drops the one he has to go for the larger bone. But, alas, it is just a reflection. That's the Clinton health plan. If we go for it, we're dumber than the dog.

Nuts and Bolts of Secession

DECEMBER 29, 1993

In an earlier column, I suggested that liberty-loving Americans begin to think about secession. That column brought in the greatest amount of reader response this year. Virtually all of it was supportive. Since then, I've discovered there are groups actually studying the matter. One is the Utah-based Committee of 50 States, chaired by former Utah governor J. Bracken Lee and directed by Professor Joseph Stumph.

Their proposal is less radical than secession. They're trying to get thirty-eight state legislatures, three-fourths of the states, to pass what they call the Ultimatum Resolution, which kicks in when the federal debt reaches $6 trillion. If the Ultimatum Resolution went into effect, it would dissolve the entire federal apparatus. The president, members of Congress and the Senate, and the federal judiciary would be summarily fired.

"Would that be constitutional?" you say. You bet it is, and here's the reasoning. At the time of our first constitutional convention, in 1787, the thirteen original states had status as sovereign, free, and independent nations. They created the federal government, delegating it certain limited powers. In other words, the federal government is an agent created by the states, who are the principals. The relationship between the states and the federal government is the same as the relationship between stockholders (principals) and a corporation (their agent). Stockholders can dissolve corporations and fire officers, directors, and CEOs. The states, as principals, allow the federal government to exist at their pleasure. Three-fourths of the states can withdraw all federal authority to act for them.

The scoundrels in Washington have it ass backward. They act as if states are a creature of the federal government. The Ultimatum Resolution anticipates Washington's appetite for control. In case Congress by treaty, or the president by Executive Order, declares a "national emergency" or otherwise attempts to suspend, abolish, or in some other manner eliminate the Constitution and Bill of Rights, the Ultimatum Resolution presents a significant barrier. It contains a provision whereby any attempt to abolish, suspend, or eliminate our Constitution would automatically cause the states to take back all delegated powers and the federal government to cease to exist. Each of the fifty states would automatically and immediately become a separate and sovereign nation, as the thirteen original states were some 210 years ago, until and if the free and independent republics came together to form a new confederation.

Of course, if thirty-eight state legislatures cannot be convinced to adopt the Ultimatum Resolution, secession by states would be the next step. You say, "Williams, secession is not right; plus, it's unlawful." History lesson: Texas seceded from Mexico, and U.S. annexation precipitated the U.S.-Mexico War of 1846. Panama seceded from Colombia with our help. While Abraham Lincoln was telling eleven Southern states they couldn't secede, he assisted and approved of West Virginia seceding from Virginia in direct violation of Article IV, Section 3, of our Constitution that says, "No new State shall be formed or erected with the jurisdiction of any other State . . . without the consent of the Legislatures of the States concerned."

Moral justification for secession is found in our Declaration of Independence. It says governments are created to protect our unalienable right to life, liberty, and the pursuit of happiness. "Whenever a government becomes destructive of these ends, it is the right of the people to alter or abolish it." But let's think about the Committee of 50 States' Ultimatum Resolution approach first.

The Road to Serfdom

JANUARY 26, 1994

People recognize my friend Thomas Sowell, senior fellow at the Hoover Institution, as a scholar who has distinguished himself in the analysis of race and ethnicity both in the United States and internationally. But that's really an add-on skill, plus a diversion, for which I am partly to blame. Sowell's real forte lies in the history of economic thought, placing him among the world's top four or five economists in that area. Nowhere has his breadth of knowledge been so concisely put than in his recent *Forbes* article (1/17/94) on the thought of Nobel laureate Friedrich Hayek.

Fifty years ago, Hayek wrote a critique of socialism bearing the title *The Road to Serfdom*. It is the most powerful, yet-to-be-refuted argument that fascism, communism, and socialism are kindred forms of collectivism whose survival critically depends on the undermining of private property rights, rule of law, limited government, and other institutions that make liberty possible. Collectivists everywhere, including American liberals, disdain the rule of law, traditions, and the marketplace in favor of the direct pursuit of results.

According to Hayek, collectivists are "dangerous idealists" who have "prepared the way for totalitarians," though they themselves are morally incapable of doing the things necessary for the preservation of the collectivist state. These "dangerous idealists" build the Trojan horse for tyrants. Or, as Sowell says, "Once you open the floodgates, you cannot tell the water where to go." If collectivism is to survive, there must be state terror to suppress dissent. In renouncing the use of state terror, Gorbachev unwittingly doomed communism and the Russian empire.

Like Hayek, Sowell doesn't spend much time criticizing the intentions of socialists because "the issue is not what anyone intends but what consequences are in fact likely to follow." Sowell says the Bush administration's Americans with Disabilities Act (ADA) and the Clinton health plan are large down payments on socialism. You say, "But, Williams, the ADA and universal medical coverage are socially good things!" That's the problem. The emphasis is on promised results, not process, as collectivists do everywhere.

Here are a few process questions: What happens to people's rights to engage in peaceable voluntary exchange? What about the principle of equality before the law and private property rights? What happens to people's rights to be free to make their own decisions? If you say those questions are not as important as achieving the results promised by the ADA and universal medical care, your vision differs only in degree (but not in kind) from that of people like Hitler, Mussolini, Stalin, and Mao Tse-tung.

Answers to the next set of questions may suggest not that much of a difference in degree. Suppose Clinton's health plan mandates fixed doctor's fees and my doctor and I agree to a higher one. Would you have me fined or jailed for committing what the Soviets called an economic crime against the state? What if I refuse to designate handicapped parking slots at my place of business, the government orders the shop closed, and I refuse? Would it be OK for armed agents to use force and shoot me if necessary? You say, "But, Williams, you're violating the law." That's right, but so were the Soviet citizens sent to the gulag.

We Americans must stop asking and allowing Congress to trash the Constitution and our liberty-enhancing institutions. If we don't, we will travel farther down the road to serfdom and meet with the same disasters of other collectivist nations.

Better yet, read Hayek's classic or at least Sowell's distillation.

The Waco Holocaust Update

FEBRUARY 9, 1994

The Indianapolis-based American Justice Federation (AJF) has released a video titled "Waco, the Big Lie." It's narrated by an obviously sympathetic Linda Thompson. Forget what she says, and just view the video. What's seen should call for an independent investigation into the official lies and cover-up about Waco. David Koresh's kooky beliefs and behavior are one thing. But if we allow Washington to get away with actions leading to the deaths of eighty-five men, women, and children, who's next?

The Clinton administration told us the four Alcohol, Tobacco and Firearms agents were killed by the Branch Davidians. The AJF video suggests that three of the agents were killed by one of their own, who is shown tossing a smoke grenade into the room fellow agents just entered and then spraying the room with machine-gun fire.

There was no justification for the paramilitary raid on Mount Carmel to arrest Koresh. The Bureau of Alcohol, Tobacco and Firearms (BATF) claimed it couldn't arrest him because he hadn't been out of the compound for months. But a waitress and a manager at a local grill said he was in the restaurant just three weeks before the raid.

The affidavit that served as the basis for BATF's search warrant and its hundred-man assault was falsified. BATF agent Davy Aguilera made several false allegations to secure the warrant. He said that Koresh had a clandestine firearms publication, which was false; that machine-gun fire was heard at the compound, false; and that there was child abuse, which was not only false but outside the jurisdiction of the BATF.

According to documentation contained in a special report of the Gun Owners Foundation, FBI and Texas Ranger sources say the BATF fired first. The Waco raid appears to be part of an official agenda to eliminate religious "cults" and as such is a part of a more generalized attack on religion in our country. Plus, there was a side dish of showboating evidenced by BATF agent Sharon Wheeler's call to editors at local ABC and NBC affiliates with the message "we have something big going down."

When scores of armed agents, as reported in the *Waco Tribune Herald*, "leap out of the cattle trucks, throwing concussion grenades and screaming 'Come out!'" what are your rights? Section 9.31 of the Texas Penal Code states, "The use of force to resist arrest or search is justified: (1) If, before the actor offers any resistance, the peace officer (or person acting at his direction) uses or attempts to use force greater than that necessary to make the arrest and search; and (2) When and to the degree the actor reasonably believes the force is immediately necessary to protect himself against the peace officer's (or other person's) use or attempted use of greater force than necessary." If the BATF had a warrant based on falsified statements and used inappropriate force, a case might be made that the Branch Davidians had every right to defend themselves just as Warsaw ghetto Jews did against the Nazi SS.

The Waco case cries for a full outside investigation, but there's a more important lesson. In the pursuit of its socialist agenda, Congress would love to have agents of bureaucracies like the Environmental Protection Agency, Fish and Wildlife, Food and Drug Administration, Internal Revenue Service, and the BATF run roughshod over our liberties and property rights. If we are unarmed, their job is a bit easier. An unarmed citizenry is a top priority on the liberal agenda. The Brady bill is the first step.

Congressional Wickedness

MARCH 30, 1994

Senator David Pryor (D-Ark.) and the first lady made names for themselves beating up on drug companies. But they and their bureaucracies, not the drug companies, are the villains. "There you go again, Williams," you say, "beating up on the honorable people we elect to office." Let's look at it.

Congress controls the Food and Drug Administration (FDA), whose stated mission is to protect us against unsafe and ineffective drugs. Because of congressionally sanctioned drug approval policy, pharmaceutical companies spend more than $231 million and twelve years to get a drug through the FDA's approval process. Studies show that the FDA's approval process doubles the cost of developing a new drug, and guess who ultimately pays?

One effect of this policy is the phenomenon of "orphan" drugs. Orphan drugs are those that might be effective in treating a disease, but the number of affected Americans is so small that the drug companies would lose money getting them through the FDA's approval process. That means people suffer needlessly. But that's politically acceptable to Congress because the victims don't know why they suffer.

According to a study done by Arthur D. Little Associates, the ten-year delay in getting approval for propranolol (a widely used beta-blocker for the treatment of angina and hypertension) to be marketed in the United States resulted in the deaths of about 100,000 Americans who might have lived had the drug been available earlier. Dr. George Hitchings, 1988 Nobel laureate in medicine, reports that the FDA delay in approving the antibacterial drug Septra cost more than 80,000 American lives.

Congressmen like Pryor and FDA officials are fully aware of these effects of their policies. But here's the scam: FDA officials can make two basic errors. They can err on the side of undercaution and approve a drug with dangerous, unanticipated side effects. Or they can err on the side of overcaution, creating costly and lengthy drug approval procedures. If they err on the side of undercaution, they'll be embarrassed, possibly losing careers and promotions, by news stories of sick people, congressional investigations, and hearings. If they err on the side of overcaution, as in the cases of propranolol, Septra, and other drugs, they go scot-free. Victims of those errors are invisible. Neither they nor their families know why they died. Which error do you think Congress and FDA officials prefer? If you said errors where victims are invisible, go to the head of the class.

This cruel policy is just one more example of the wickedness of Congress and its bureaucrats. Instead of demanding that these charlatans and hustlers get out of our lives, too many Americans want to give them greater control. They seem to want Congress to do to our total health care system what they've done to pharmaceuticals, the deficit, national debt, schools, and criminals. I just plain don't get it. Are we Americans stupid or just eternally optimistic?

Back to drugs. There's a need to ensure drug safety and effectiveness. Recognition of that fact doesn't mean that the FDA is the best way. Safety certification could be done privately as the Underwriters Laboratory certifies the safety of electrical equipment and appliances. "But, Williams," you ask, "should profit-motivated private companies be entrusted with such an important task?" Let me put it back on you. Whom do you trust most to safely deliver parcels: UPS, FedEx, or the Postal Service? Whom do you trust most with the safety and education of your kids: private schools or government ones? Whom do you trust most with your own life: a Veterans Administration hospital or a private hospital?

A Deficit and Debt Cure

MARCH 16, 1994

Politicians love to posture and moan about debt and deficits. But are they serious? This week, they have the opportunity to put their money where their mouth is—or is it our money where their mouth is? Representative Jon Kyl (R-Ariz.) introduced the Balanced Budget/Spending Limitation Amendment (BBSLA) as a substitute for Charles Stenholm's Balanced Budget Amendment, whose Senate version went down to defeat. The Kyl amendment is cosponsored by seventy-one congressmen, including the half dozen or so whom our founding fathers would respect such as Representatives Dick Armey, Chris Cox, Tom DeLay, and Dana Rohrabacher.

Section 1 of the amendment says, "A fiscal year's expenditures shall not exceed that fiscal year's revenues." That requirement alone doesn't do a thing for our liberty or fiscal sanity. After all, our gross national product is $6 trillion a year. Who'd be happy if federal expenditures were $6 trillion and federal tax revenues were $6 trillion? A balanced budget requirement alone would permit Congress to continue its spending spree. Congressmen would be within the law if they constantly raised taxes to match it.

It's Section 2 of Kyl's amendment that gives it piranha-like teeth and as such creates dim prospects for passage: "A fiscal year's expenditures shall not exceed 19 percent of that year's gross national product" (GNP). The reasoning is that 19 percent of the GNP is the average federal revenues collected over the last forty years, despite good or bad economic times or tax rate increases or decreases. The spending limitation mandate would eliminate congressional hotdogging with our earnings. The bill gives Congress incentive to enact growth policies; that's the only way it'd get more money to spend.

The bill has an emergency provision. On the declaration of an emergency, the balanced budget/spending limitation requirement could be waived for a single year by a three-fifths vote of both houses of Congress. Plus, there's a presidential pork killer—a line-item veto.

Kyl's proposal is the best thing going so far and would go a long way toward reining in congressional spending. But suppose there were a congressman named Williams, what would he add to the Kyl amendment to give it even more teeth? The first addition would be a section saying that the federal government shall not directly or indirectly require states, local governments, and persons to engage in additional activities without federal compensation to cover those additional costs. That would take care of congressional unfunded mandates that are bankrupting state and local governments and individuals.

"Congressman" Williams's second addition would be that of giving any member of Congress standing before the U.S. District Court of Washington, D.C., so that he or she could bring an action enforcing the amendment. Right now, Congress is not obliged to obey all laws, even its own laws.

"Williams," you say, "why hamstring Congress? Don't you trust them?" I trust Congress about as much as the framers did. Read the Constitution and its first ten amendments. You will find negative words and phrases like "shall not," "not," and "disparage" at least fifty times. The framers held a deep distrust of Congress. Indeed, after departing this world, it's a guarantee that you've arrived in hell if you see anything resembling our Bill of Rights. Such a document in heaven would be an insult to a merciful and just God. And speaking of religion, I plan to ask Kyl why he settled for 19 percent. If 10 percent is good enough for the Baptist Church, how come it's not good enough for Congress?

Worthless Laws

May 11, 1994

Would you have condemned a 1940s German citizen for disobeying Nazi laws against concealing and sheltering Jews? What about the South African businessmen who hired black workers in certain jobs in flagrant violation of the country's apartheid laws? Would you have called for the arrest of pre–Civil War whites who violated fugitive slave laws by assisting runaway slaves? "OK, Williams," you say, "the answer is no! But what's the point?" It's easy. Immoral laws aren't worthy of obedience. French philosopher Frederic Bastiat said, "When law and morality contradict each other, the citizen has the cruel alternative of either losing his moral sense or losing his respect for the law." Blind obedience to immoral laws is itself immoral.

Not every constitution is as steeped in morality as ours is. However, our Constitution has been under siege by an immoral Congress, abetted by a derelict Supreme Court. The Constitution is quite clear about the relationship between the people, the state, and the federal government. The Tenth Amendment says, "The powers not delegated to the United States by the Constitution nor prohibited by it to the states, are reserved to the States respectively, or to the people." Despite that clear, unambiguous statement, states and local jurisdictions can do little without federal permission. Besides, they're faced with hundreds of costly federal mandates that range from meeting requirements of the Americans with Disabilities Act to Environmental Protection Agency mandates for asbestos removal. Not only do many federal mandates serve little useful purpose, they're also unfunded and are driving otherwise fiscally prudent states, cities, and localities into bankruptcy.

Fortunately, some Americans are responding to Washington's heavy hand. State of Colorado legislators Charles Duke and Jim Roberts introduced House Joint Resolution 94. It passed in both houses and now awaits the governor's signature. The resolution, now HR 1035, in part reads: "The scope of power defined by the 10th Amendment means that the federal government was created by the states specifically to be an agent of the states. . . . Whereas, many federal mandates are directly in violation of the 10th Amendment. . . . Whereas, The U.S. Supreme Court has ruled in New York vs. United States (1992) that Congress may not simply commandeer the legislative and regulatory processes of the states. Resolved, the State of Colorado hereby claims sovereignty under the 10th Amendment, [and] the federal government, as our agent, is hereby instructed to cease and desist, effective immediately, mandates that are beyond the scope of its authority under the 10th Amendment to the Constitution of the United States."

A similar measure has been drafted or introduced in seventeen other states. Suppose Congress ignores Colorado's resolution, should Coloradans, and citizens of other states who might pass similar resolutions, sit on their butts and whimper? Williams says no! First, citizens should sign petitions informing their state and local elected representatives that they fully support the demand that Congress obey the Tenth Amendment. Then states should give Congress an opportunity to do right by notifying it that states will not obey further mandates. If Congress persists, states should call out the National Guard and private citizens should organize militia to serve eviction notices to federal agencies in their states charged with the responsibility of violating the Tenth Amendment.

You say, "Williams, that's some pretty radical stuff; let's wait a while to see whether we can reason with them first." I'd say that most congressmen are beyond reason, but, more important, we'd better consider acting before Congress completes its agenda to disarm us through weakening our Second Amendment protections.

Expanded Opportunities

MAY 18, 1994

For years, Leroy Jones, Ani Ebong, Rowland Nwankwo, and Girma Molalegne wanted to start their own taxi company in Denver. But the Colorado Public Utilities Commission (PUC), which regulates taxis in the state, has kept them out. Acting on the behalf of entrenched taxi interests, the PUC requires new entrants to show "public need and necessity" to obtain a license. When Jones et al., or for that matter anyone else, showed up at PUC hearings, they faced a battery of high-powered lawyers hired by incumbent taxi companies to protest their getting a license. Since 1947, the Colorado PUC has not seen a "public need and necessity" for even a single new licensee.

In 1993, the Washington-based Institute for Justice brought suit against the monopolistic practices of the Colorado PUC and lost. But the resulting publicity brought a statewide call for changes in the state-backed taxicab monopoly. Last month, the Colorado legislature passed Senate Bill 113, which breaks Denver's taxi monopoly. Leroy Jones and his partners are ready to launch Freedom Cabs as soon as the governor signs the bill into law. Chip Mellor, president and general counsel for the Institute of Justice, said, "This law creates a brighter future for

Colorado entrepreneurs and consumers, and a ray of hope for those throughout America whose economic liberty is denied."

The Landmark Legal Foundation produced a similar ray of hope on the transportation front in Houston. From 1983 to 1984, Alfredo Santos, using a leased taxi, provided jitney services in the predominantly Hispanic section of east Houston. He drove along a fixed route, charging passengers a dollar for up to a five-mile trip. Santos discontinued the illegal jitney operation after having been threatened by a city official with the loss of his license to operate a taxi. Landmark represented Santos in a suit against the city of Houston to have the 1924 antijitney ordinance declared unconstitutional on the grounds that it violated antitrust laws and Santos's equal protection rights.

The U.S. District Court of Texas found Houston's antijitney ordinance, which was written as a collusive agreement between its now-defunct trolley car company and the city, was indeed unconstitutional and ruled that the city may no longer enforce it.

Indianapolis has an onerous taxi monopoly ordinance limiting the number of taxis, rigging prices, and making it all but impossible for drivers to cruise to pick up passengers. Like Houston, the ordinance bans jitney services. Mayor Stephen Goldsmith is trying to get it repealed through City County Council Proposal 72. Dick Hunt, a Republican bigwig, owner of most of the city's cabs, and giver of free rides to local politicians, presents a formidable foe to open entry. In the name of decency, let's hope the Indianapolis City County Council opts for liberty.

Government-backed transportation monopolies produce a heavy burden in low-income, high-crime minority neighborhoods. Licensed cabs are reluctant to do business in these neighborhoods, making it more difficult for residents to work and run errands. Moreover, the monopolies tend to make past discriminatory practices permanent. In the past blacks were denied licenses because of race. Now they're denied licenses because they can't prove "public need and necessity" or get together $140,000, as required in New York City to purchase a license from someone who already owns one.

There is a compelling governmental purpose for taxi, limousine, and jitney regulation. And if Williams were in charge, the questions to an applicant would be (1) Can you drive safely? (2) Is your vehicle safe? (3) Do you have passenger liability insurance? Affirmative an-

swers would win regulatory approval to enter. Any other entry requirement serves no societal purpose and constitutes monopolistic practices.

Political Arrogance and Conceit

June 8, 1994

Forget for a moment the pros and cons offered for the various health
care plans. Just keep in mind there is no free lunch. Whether Clinton
gets employee or employer mandates for health insurance, the bottom
line is that you pay. This is easily proven. Pretend you hire me. We
agree to a daily pay of $100. In addition to that cost, you must pay $8
in Social Security taxes and $12 in health insurance. Therefore, your
cost to hire me is $120 a day. Question: If you're to stay in business,
what's the minimum value that I must produce for you each day? If you
said at least $120 worth, go to the head of the class. Next question: If
I produce $120 worth of value each day, who is it that pays for Social
Security and health insurance? If you said, "Williams does!" you get an
A for Econ 101.

Continuing the scenario: The $12-a-day health insurance comes to
$3,120 a year. Suppose a person, just out of college and in good health,
prefers risking doing without health insurance. He thinks that if he
invested that money into computers and related equipment, he might
be able to develop a genetics software program that would predict a
person's future illness based on his characteristics today.

The business idea doesn't have to be so esoteric. The person might
have an imaginative idea of how to build a low-cost landscaping business. By saving $3,120 a year, after a couple of years he could self-
finance the equipment necessary to get started. You don't have to know
much business history to learn that people like the Bloomingdales,
Penneys, Roebuck, Fuller, and Madam Walker started out financing
themselves with a pittance, took risks, and became wealthy and successful by providing great services to the public.

Advocates of Clinton's health care plan, by their coercive actions,
are in effect telling unknown entrepreneurs of today that purchasing

health insurance is the best possible use for the $3,120 portion of their earnings. That's what the late Nobel laureate economist Friedrich Hayek called the "pretense of knowledge" and "fatal conceit." How can Clinton and Congress possibly know that the purchase of health insurance is a person's best use of the $3,120 portion of his earnings? How many good things for society will go undone because of Congress and Clinton's pretense of knowledge?

There are benefits to mandating that everyone have health insurance. But benefits are only a part of decision making; we must also look at costs, and those costs are not always measured in dollars. Some advocate these mandates as a means to help poor people. These people should consider that health insurance mandates have the identical effects to raising the minimum wage: further pricing low-skilled workers out of the market.

You say, "OK, Williams, that freedom stuff is OK, but if people don't have health insurance, and they get sick or injured, they become a burden on society." That's true, but it is not a problem associated with freedom; it's a problem of socialism. If I take risks resulting in untoward consequences, it is not your or anybody else's responsibility to take care of me—at least not in a free society. I must make do on charity or do without. And, by the way, medical charity has served us pretty well throughout our history.

I'd love to see Congress and Clinton debate and produce the evidence that expenditures on health insurance are the best use for each and every worker's pay. If they fail in that, they should show how their scheme is authorized by any reasonable interpretation of the U.S. Constitution.

Liberty Updates

JUNE 15, 1994

The great thing about Americans is that we don't do the wrong thing for a long period of time. Somehow, we manage to regain our wits. A few weeks back, I wrote about the sterling efforts of State of Colorado legislators Charles Duke and Jim Roberts, who introduced and successfully passed House Joint Resolution 1035, which in part reads "The scope of power defined by the 10th Amendment means that the federal government was created by the states specifically to be an agent of the states. . . . Resolved, the State of Colorado hereby claims sovereignty under the 10th Amendment, [and] the federal government, as our agent, is hereby instructed to cease and desist, effective immediately, mandates that are beyond the scope of its authority under the 10th Amendment to the Constitution of the United States."

The resolution has been given teeth. Colorado recently enacted SB-157, the Federal Mandates Act. It requires that each state agency, when making a budget request for a state program authorized or mandated by federal statute, cite specific constitutional, federal, or state provisions that authorize the program. For example, if an agency asks for money to comply with the Brady bill, the Endangered Species Act, the federal school lunch program, or a host of other federal mandates, the agency has to cite the constitutional authority. I can't wait for the fur to fly. And it will because I can't even find the word *lunch* in the U.S. Constitution. If a few dozen states pass similar legislation, it will be our best chance for a peaceful return to constitutional government.

Then there's HR 3261, introduced by Representative James A. Traficant (D-Ohio), a congressman I'd personally like to box—that is, after we determine whether Henry Waxman accepts the challenge made during my guest hosting for the honeymooning Rush Limbaugh. But Traficant's right this time. His bill would serve notice to the Internal Revenue Service (IRS) that it bears the burden of proving that a taxpayer is guilty of filing a fraudulent tax return. Everywhere, except in a tax court, a basic tenet of our justice system is that a defendant is innocent until proven guilty. The necessity for Traficant's bill is a sad commentary about tax court judges. Don't all judges have a sworn duty to place the burden of proof on plaintiffs?

HR 3261 also raises IRS liability if it recklessly or intentionally disregards a taxpayer's rights. Under current law, taxpayers may sue for up to $100,000 in damages. Traficant's bill raises it to $1 million. In addition, HR 3261 allows the court to assess a monetary penalty to those agents who are found to disregard taxpayer's rights.

But HR 3261 has been prevented from reaching the House of Representatives' floor for a vote. It's bottled up in the powerful Ways and

Means Committee. And who's the king of Ways and Means? It's none other than Dan Rostenkowski, the congressman under criminal indictment for long-term, big-time theft of taxpayer money. When Rosty has his day in court, he's going to want the burden of proof to be on the plaintiff. But for us as taxpayers before his agents, he sees it a different way. What else is new about our political scoundrels?

So far, 101 congressmen have signed a discharge petition to get HR 3261 out of the Ways and Means Committee and to the floor for a vote. In order for the discharge petition to succeed, 117 more congressmen must sign. I wonder why more congressmen won't sign—could they, in an effort to squeeze more tax dollars out of us, support IRS tactics?

Hamstring Government

July 27, 1994

Congressman Dick Armey (R-Tex.) says, "Our government is too big—[it] spends, taxes and regulates too much." Then, in his article published in the June 13, 1994, issue of the *Wall Street Journal*, he goes on to say why and offer solutions.

Today, the average family pays more in taxes than for food, clothing, and shelter combined. More than 40 percent of the nation's annual income is spent by politicians rather than by the people who earned it. But that's just part of our congressionally imposed burden. Taxpayers must keep records, decipher the tax code, employ accountants, and find legal ways to reduce their tax burden. That comes to seven billion hours each year simply complying with the code. If the hours spent complying with the tax code were put to productive work, they'd represent the entire annual outputs of the U.S. auto, truck, and aircraft industries.

Therefore, Armey has introduced HR 4585, the Freedom and Fairness Restoration Act. If this bill, modeled after a plan developed by Hoover Institution economists Robert Hall and Alvin Rabushka in 1981, becomes law, we'd be able to file our income taxes on a postcard. HR 4585 provides that all personal income be taxed at a single rate of 17 percent. There would be a $5,300 deduction for each child.

There are provisions for a $13,000 individual deduction, $17,200 for a single head of household, and $26,200 for a married couple. Individual and single head-of-household deductions would have the effect of taking poor households off the tax rolls.

Business taxes could be handled just as simply.

Business would subtract expenses from revenue and pay 17 percent of the difference (profits) as taxes.

Taxpayers don't fully appreciate Congress's tax gouging because they never actually see their full paycheck. Because of withholding the "temporary" World War II Victory Tax, Congress has been able to sock it to us without our paying a lot of attention. Armey's bill would eliminate tax withholding. Just as we do with our other bills, we'd be required to write a monthly check to the government to cover our tax liabilities.

Armey's bill also mandates that federal spending be frozen at 1994 levels with an inflation adjustment. This would eliminate $475 billion worth of projected spending increases. All unearned entitlement programs would have a life of ten years. Then Congress would have to review them and vote for renewal. Another positive feature of Armey's bill is that federal agencies would be required to make a cost-benefit analysis of regulatory mandates, which are really a form of massive hidden taxes. Plus, agencies like the Environmental Protection Agency and Fish and Wildlife Services would be forced to compensate property owners when they make regulations that significantly reduce the value of property.

Dick Armey, formerly a professor of economics, is one of the six or seven members of Congress who would be respected by the framers of the Constitution. The framers would see the rest of Congress as people contemptuous of constitutional principles and bereft of any sense of morality. That's why there's little chance that Armey's colleagues will enact this legislation. Why? A simplified tax code denies congressmen the opportunity to exchange tax privileges for votes and campaign contributions. It would reduce their ability to micromanage our lives through granting tax write-offs for this and tax penalties for that. Because the House Ways and Means and the Senate Finance Committees are in charge of taxes, congressmen salivate at the prospect of becoming a member and acquiring power perks.

Unless we hamstring Washington, we are going to lose liberty and prosperity. Armey's Freedom and Fairness Restoration Act is a start.

Congressionally Mandated Nightmares

SEPTEMBER 28, 1994

How about a few tidbits you're not likely to hear about elsewhere that raise costs, reduce choices, and show how a foolish, know-it-all Congress interferes with our lives?

A Southern California dry cleaner was fined $250 for not posting the number of employees injured in the previous twelve months. But there were no employee injuries. Thus, the business was fined for simply not posting a blank sheet of paper.

The Environmental Protection Agency (EPA) fined a North Carolina subsidiary of the Marmon Group $5,000 for inadvertently writing the company's name on line 17 rather than line 18 of a form. The EPA imposed $600,000 in fines and legal fees on another subsidiary of the Marmon Group for failing to fill out a federal form, even though the company complied with the identical state law.

The Food and Drug Administration passed a new rule requiring McCurdy Fish Company of Lubeck, Maine, to gut freshly caught fish before immersing them in brine tanks. Unable to bear the additional cost, John McCurdy shut his plant down, laying off all twenty-two workers. This was after twenty years in business and not a single case of botulism reported against McCurdy.

The U.S. Army Corps of Engineers fined a Minnesota farmer $45,000 for filling in a one-acre glacial pothole that was making farming difficult on his property. Having fined him, the corps made him dig the fill out.

A Maryland couple suffered devastating financial losses when the endangered puritan tiger beetle was found on their property. To protect the beetle, the couple was prohibited from taking action to halt the soil erosion that was jeopardizing their home. During their fight with federal agents, 22 feet of their property plunged into the Chesapeake Bay.

Tuang Ming Lin, a Vietnam refugee, faces one year in prison and a $300,000 fine because federal agents accused him of running over "five suspected Tipton kangaroo rats" while tilling his 719-acre farm in Bakersfield, California. Federal agents have already seized his $50,000 tractor.

If you think our only constitutional guarantee not yet usurped by Congress is the Third Amendment protection against the quartering of troops, think again. It is under siege. But it's animals and insects we must quarter instead of soldiers. There's a Western solution to this aspect of congressional heavy-handedness. If you spot an endangered species on your land, shoot, shovel, and shut up.

Michael Rowe broke the law when he built a firebreak around his Riverside, California, house. His house was saved while most of his neighbors lost theirs in the fires that erupted in Southern California last year. It's that kangaroo rat again. Acting on the demands of environmentalists to protect the kangaroo rat, Congress prevented homeowners from building firebreaks in or around the rat habitat. This is yet another example of invisible victims of congressional policy: Devastated homeowners blamed the fires and winds instead of the environmentalists and Congress.

That's on California's destruction side. In 1993, $500 million in construction was halted in Orange County, California, by the Fish and Wildlife Service to protect the 2-inch Pacific pocket mouse.

This is just a sampling of congressional folly compiled by the Washington-based Americans for Tax Reform Foundation. We can't just stop Congress from doing stupid things; we must eliminate its capacity to do so. First, we must force Congress to respect the Tenth Amendment and, second, reduce its financial resources by limiting what it can spend.

Deception 101

July 13, 1994

Philosopher David Hume said, "It is seldom that liberty of any kind is lost all at once." The "why" is easy. Tyrants know they'd meet stronger resistance that way. When you're trying to get something over on somebody, it pays to do it in degrees. And that's what the recent Senate Finance Committee socialized health bill agreement is about. Thinking of Bill Clinton's alleged strategy in another setting, we should name that agreement "just kiss it," JKI for short. But before I'm accused of being overly cynical, let's have a little history about JKI strategy.

During the 1913 legislative debate on the income tax, Congress promised that the top tax rate would never exceed 7 percent and that was on incomes over $500,000 (more than $5.5 million in today's dollars). The personal exemption for a single person was $3,000 ($34,400 in today's dollars) and for a married couple $4,000 ($45,900 today). In 1913, only 4 percent of the American population earned enough to file a tax return. The Sixteenth Amendment would have never been ratified had Congress sought the tax code we have today back then. It was a JKI.

How about Social Security taxes? Back in 1933, during their legislative debates, congressmen promised that no one would ever pay more than $60, $120 tops, a year in Social Security taxes; moreover, a person's benefits would be tied to what he put in. Now, Social Security taxes are higher than income taxes for the average wage earner. Another JKI.

When cigarette prohibitionists started out, they didn't call for bans on smoking in airplanes, restaurants, offices, factories, sports arenas, and restrooms. Neither did they call for confiscatory taxes on cigarettes. They did a JKI and demanded no-smoking sections on airplanes.

That brings us back to the health care bill. The Senate Finance Committee's agreement says, "No employer or individual would be forced to buy insurance, although universal coverage is a national goal." That's a JKI.

It goes on to say, "If insurance reforms, subsidies and other measures fail to cover 95 percent of Americans by 2002, the national health commission would recommend action." Another JKI.

"Standard plans would include abortion, but any employer or health plan could refuse to buy or offer abortion coverage." Both the Senate Finance Committee and the House Ways and Means Committee versions of socialized medicine plans are loaded with provisions that won't be enacted now but leave the door open for onerous mandates later.

And if you don't believe Congress will come through that door, you're probably in the class of people who actually believed that the income tax would never be more than 7 percent, Social Security taxes wouldn't exceed $60 or $120 a year, cigarette prohibitionists only wanted no-smoking sections on planes, and the World War II Victory Tax, mandating withholding of income taxes, was just a temporary measure.

If Republican members of Congress had one scintilla of sense or courage, they would back away from any measure that socializes and hence damages a medical system that leads the world in innovation, education, and delivery of services. We do have problems in our medical system. But most of them stem from one form or another of government intervention. We solve those problems by reducing government's role, not by enlarging it.

In any case, we should be at least as smart as Paula Jones. When somebody asks you to just kiss it, you know that person has more in mind. So if you don't want to go all the way, run like hell.

Growing Contempt for Government

OCTOBER 19, 1994

Rush Limbaugh has more than five million listeners a day. G. Gordon Liddy might have a couple of million. Baltimore's Alan Keyes, a radio talk show newcomer, has recently become syndicated. Then there's Los Angeles's Errol Smith and Larry Elder, Denver's Ken Hamblin, and Washington's Armstrong Williams. Limbaugh and Liddy are white guys, and Keyes, Smith, Elder, Hamblin, and Williams are black guys. What they and a growing number of popular conservative talk shows have in common is that they've become forums for millions of Americans fed up with government and politicians.

Callers are ordinary Americans trying to earn a living, pay their bills, and raise their families. Many are just about ready to reject the legitimacy of the federal government. They're paying more in federal taxes than for food, shelter, and clothing combined and increasingly see themselves victimized by government. Their grievance list includes men victimized by sex quotas, whites victimized by race quotas, blacks victimized by fraudulent schools and rampant crime, small businessmen victimized by regulations, devoutly religious people compelled to pay for abortions and pornography, gun owners who see politicians taking them on and turning criminals loose, and smokers who are made to feel like social outcasts.

For the most part, talk radio audiences are the people who make this country work, who are being forcibly used to serve the purposes of the tax eaters. Politicians and bureaucrats, being tax eaters, along with their sycophants in the news media, have contempt for both the hosts and their audiences.

Ordinary law-abiding Americans have become targets for vicious government harassment that ranges from having to comply with stupid and costly environmental and endangered species regulations to what is no less than government-sponsored massacre in Waco, Texas. While decent Americans have become government targets, criminals and bums, deviants of every stripe have become society's mascots to be coddled with sensitivity, their "rights" worshiped and paraded before us as moral equivalents on *Oprah* and *Donahue*.

Decent people are tired of being criminalized. That's precisely what Congress does every day—criminalizes Americans by turning previously peaceable voluntary transactions into criminal acts. If Congress and Clinton have their way in socializing our health care system, they will add to that health criminals. What is not a criminal act now—choosing your doctor and paying him out of your pocket—will become criminal.

The most important contribution of talk radio is that it has reduced feelings of isolation. Americans who have been victimized by one government policy or another have felt alone and guilty. If they are against race and sex quotas, intellectual elites, politicians, and the news media made them feel like they're racists and sexists. If they smoke, they are made to feel like the personification of evil. If they are against unconstitutional gun control, they're made to feel guilty for America's crime. But talk radio lets people know they are not by themselves; they're in the company of millions.

Large numbers of Americans are just about ready to declare themselves innocent. They are coming to realize that it's an illegitimate Congress and that many laws it writes are unjust. Like our founders, they're beginning to conclude there's no moral duty to obey unjust laws. They see government, especially Washington, as the enemy. If Congress continues to underestimate the level of deep-seated anger across the land and presses on with its agenda to control, things are going to heat up. The fact that today's Americans have unprecedented moral contempt for both the incumbent president and Congress won't make it any better.

Don't Tread on Me

NOVEMBER 9, 1994

Without question, Americans have known unprecedented liberty. But increasingly, we're trading liberty for safety—somewhat like a caged canary. If ignorance rather than design explains our headlong rush toward tyranny and servitude, there's hope for us. So let me share some liberty tidbits from Lysander Spooner (1808–87), one of my early American heroes (his collection is available from Laissez-Faire Books).

Spooner argued that all people are endowed with equal rights to life, liberty, and property, adding that these "natural rights are inalienable and can no more be surrendered to government, which is but an association of individuals, than to a single individual." This vision inspired Spooner to write *Unconstitutionality of Slavery* and later *A Defence for Fugitive Slaves*. He advanced the brilliant argument that would become known as *jury nullification*—that juries are legally sovereign. As such, juries have the right to judge a defendant not guilty if it judges the law, even if it has been upheld by the Supreme Court, to be defective, unwarranted, or wrongly applied. Thus, Spooner argued, because slavery itself was unjust, the newly enacted fugitive slave law was unjust and juries should exonerate all accused of violating it. Today's juries still have the common law right of nullification, but the thugs sitting on the bench either deny or don't inform juries of that right.

Suppose you see Williams making lots of money as a gigolo. Would you have him arrested? Has a crime been committed? First, what's a crime? Spooner says, "Crimes are those acts by which one man harms the person or property of another." Prostitution is a vice, and Spooner says, "Vices are simply the errors which a man makes in his search after his own happiness." He adds, "It is a maxim of law that there can be no crime without criminal intent; that is, without the intent to invade the person or property of another."

"Hold it, Williams," you say. "Any violation of a law is a crime and warrants punishment." You're wrong. For the government to declare a vice a crime is to violate those natural law guarantees of life, liberty, and pursuit of happiness, which are enunciated in our Declaration of Independence. Spooner says only a fool or an impostor believes that he as an individual has the right to punish other men for their vices. Therefore, government cannot have a right that individuals do not have. For example, individuals don't have the right to murder and steal—and therefore cannot give government that right. Individuals do have the right to protect their property and punish violators; therefore, they can grant such a right to government.

These principles of natural law that played such an important role in the framers' thinking about our Constitution are held in high contempt by Congress, the courts, and, I'm afraid, most Americans. My deepest lifetime disappointment is the fact that black Americans share so much of this generalized contempt and eagerly advocate and participate in the attack against the principles of natural law. Blacks, more than any other Americans, should love and respect natural law and have the deepest suspicions of government. After all, the horrors of slavery and the abuses of Reconstruction and Jim Crow were rooted in disrespect for natural law.

The good news is there's a ray of hope on the horizon directly proportional to the growing arrogance of Congress. It's the emerging leave-me-alone attitude developing across the land. The founders might have called it "Don't tread on me!"

The Third Rebellion

November 23, 1994

Standing on the Gettysburg battlefield two weekends ago, I had mixed feelings about just what the war settled. The good news is that the war between the states finally settled the issue of slavery that had threatened the formation of the union in the first place. The bad news is that the war also settled the question of secession.

Among those truths the framers held as self-evident is that "whenever any form of government becomes destructive of these ends [human rights to life, liberty, and pursuit of happiness], it is the right of the people to alter or to abolish it, and to institute new government." The framers recognized that people have the right to fight tyranny and that collections of people have the right to secede from a tyrannical government. After all, the Declaration of Independence was a declaration of secession from the tyranny of King George.

Federal suppression of the Southern rebellion settled the question of the right to secede. With that accomplished, the federal government was free to trash the Tenth Amendment and the states are left whistling "Dixie." "That's not quite true, Williams," you say. "There's the Supreme Court to protect the Tenth Amendment." Nonsense! If you're seeking protection for the Tenth Amendment, you'd be better off in a kangaroo court.

The federal government's riding roughshod over our basic liberties, plus states' not having the right to secede, increases the potential for human conflict. It's like marriage without the right to divorce. What alternatives would a mate have against a spouse who's broken every oath and is brutal to boot? If you said, "Fight back," go to the head of the class.

Fighting back and preparation for armed resistance are what's beginning to happen, particularly in the West, and for good reason. Article I, Section 8, of our Constitution permits the federal government to exercise "authority over all places purchased by the consent of the legislature of the state . . . for the erection of forts, magazines, arsenals, dockyards and other needful buildings." That statement is easy to understand. So how does it translate into the federal government controlling 86 percent of the land in Nevada and similarly high proportions in Alaska, Utah, New Mexico, and California?

I applaud citizens in Nevada, New Mexico, and Utah who are fighting back. Nye County commissioner Richard Carver has issued a declaration saying that all public lands in Nye County belong to the state of Nevada. Citizens have begun to ignore the dictates of the U.S. Forest Service. Elsewhere, Montana citizens have begun a serious secession movement. In Michigan, Texas, Ohio, and Louisiana, honest and law-abiding citizens are forming armed militias.

As the recent elections have shown, more and more Americans have become increasingly tired of being taxed and regulated to death. Congress has destructively intruded into nearly every aspect of our lives. Arrogant politicians have forced us to pay for activities that many of us deem ungodly and evil. In the process, they have made a complete mockery of our social contract—the Constitution and the Bill of Rights. Today's Americans have just as many, if not more, grievances as our founders had against King George. If we can believe recent Republican Party rhetoric, there is a window of opportunity left open to avoid inevitable conflict. If the new Republican leadership has a modicum of character and statesmanship, after they take their oaths of office to uphold the Constitution, they will move to repeal any and all federal regulations that violate it. Will you please hold your breath with me?

Send a Real Message

OCTOBER 26, 1994

You'd have to be dumb, deaf, and blind not to know that Americans have reached an all-time low in their respect for Congress and government in general. And they're right. Government is the cause of most of what's wrong in America. It has crippled productivity growth, waged an immoral war against honest, moral citizens, confiscated our earnings at an unprecedented pace, and made a mockery of our Constitution.

I share this contempt for Congress, but I'm ready to put my money where my mouth is; are you? Let's look at it. Representative Tom Foley (D-Wash.), Speaker of the House of Representatives, is up for reelection. He's in deep political trouble with his voters. He's sued to block a term limitation initiative approved by Washington State voters and supported President Clinton's efforts to socialize our health care system despite the wishes of most Americans. Many of his constituents see him as an arrogant tyrant. So what's his strategy to add two more years to his already thirty in Congress? It's to remind his constituents that it was his clout that got federal money to widen highways in his district and his clout that spared the shutdown of Fairchild Air Force Base and that he's going to deliver more pork if reelected.

According to a story in USA Today (9/29/94), a few of his constituents argue that Foley's clout outweighs the benefits of sending a message to Washington: "He's very powerful, and it would be foolish to throw him out." The point here is not to single out Foley; the argument to vote him back in provides a concrete example of the cancer that grips our nation. Americans seem to have adopted the attitude that differs little from saying it's OK for their congressman to promote legislation that is destructive to our country so long as he brings back highway construction funds, keeps their local military installation open, and raids the Treasury for other constituent interests.

Foley's constituents can make impassioned pleas about the jobs and "military importance" of Fairchild Air Force Base as well as their other local interests. But Senator Arlen Specter's (R-Pa.) constituents can make similar pleas about the jobs and "military importance" of the Philadelphia Naval Base, highway construction, and raids on the Treasury.

The problem is that there are 535 congressmen and senators and their constituents who can make similarly persuasive arguments for raids on the federal Treasury. Their skill in making those arguments helps explain why we face unprecedented national debt, unprecedented budget deficits, and federal government run amok. Whether we want to acknowledge it or not, we have become a nation of thieves. We use our elected representatives in an effort to steal from one another, albeit a legalized form of theft. And from a strictly economic point of view, once legalized theft becomes institutionalized, it pays for all of us to strive to get our share just to make ourselves whole.

Next month, we have a midterm election. If Americans really want to send a message of disgust about what's happening to our country, we're going to see what we've never seen before.

Congressmen are going to be out there campaigning on their record of bringing back goodies. Choruses of boos will arise from their constituents and chants like "Because we're moral and obey moral rules, we do not accept stolen goods." I'd love to see that, and if we don't, how much you want to bet that future generations will curse our memory?

Recovering Our Liberties

NOVEMBER 2, 1994

"The Powers not delegated to the United States by the Constitution, nor prohibited by it to the States, are reserved to the States respectively, or to the people." That's the clear message of the now-meaningless Tenth Amendment to our Constitution. However, California has just joined Colorado, Missouri, Hawaii, and Illinois in asserting Tenth Amendment rights, demanding that the federal government cease and desist all mandates and interferences exceeding those delegated by the Constitution. Under the leadership of California State senator Don Rogers, Senate Joint Resolution 44, claiming state sovereignty under the Tenth Amendment, won approval in the California Assembly by a vote of fifty-four to twelve and in the state Senate by twenty-two to nine. Similar resolutions are in the introduction or drafting stage in protest against the heavy-handed mandates and edicts of Congress.

Were it not for the Tenth Amendment, our founders would have never ratified the Constitution. They correctly feared consolidation, the development of a powerful and meddlesome federal government. James Madison explained Washington's role in *The Federalist Papers*: "The powers delegated by the proposed Constitution to the federal government are few and defined. Those which are to remain in the State governments are numerous and indefinite. The former will be exercised principally on external objects, as war, peace, negotiation, and foreign commerce. . . . The powers reserved to the several States will extend to all the objects which in the ordinary course of affairs, concern the lives and liberties, and properties of the people, and the internal order, improvement and prosperity of the State."

The meaning of the Tenth Amendment is clear. Our power-hungry Congress and derelict Supreme Court have allowed Madison's vision to be stood on its head so that today the powers of the federal government are "numerous and indefinite" and those of the state are "few."

The Tenth Amendment movement may be America's last chance to peacefully get Congress to obey the Constitution. Politicians have seriously underestimated public anger and are blind to the rebellion spreading across the land. In response to the heavy hand of the U.S. Forest Service, New Mexico's Catron County officials enacted the U.S. Constitution as a county ordinance and put federal officials on notice that before they even dared to breathe in Catron County they'd better show up at the supervisor's meeting to get permission. Following Catron County's lead, five other New Mexico counties, every Utah county, and Clark County and Siskiyou County in Nevada have begun resisting congressional and bureaucratic tyranny.

Tens of thousands of Americans are discussing and forming armed militia units. They are not kooks but law-abiding people who wish to be left alone by an increasingly illegitimate and meddlesome government. The government response is predictable. According to an *Albuquerque Tribune* (8/3/93) report, U.S. Forest Service ranger Mike Gardner told Catron citizens, maybe with Waco on his mind, "What are you guys arming against? A 30-30 won't do any good against Bradley fighting vehicles and attack helicopters." Gardner should have been reminded that earlier patriots took on Great Britain, the mightiest nation at that time, and won.

Like our founders, we should first peacefully petition by getting thirty-eight state legislatures to enact Tenth Amendment resolutions and put teeth in them by giving a broad outline of mandates and edicts we refuse to meet. If Congress doesn't listen, we shouldn't eschew the language tyrants understand best.

Leviathan Run Amok

DECEMBER 8, 1994

The *Kansas City Journal*'s lead article (11/24/94) tells part of the story behind the Republican midterm election sweep. There's a lot of well-justified anger resulting from stupid laws written by a wicked Congress enforced by evil, power-hungry bureaucrats. Look at just some of them.

Regulators ordered a Kansas City bank to install a braille keypad, costing $5,000, on its drive-through automatic teller machine. Steve

Mauer, the bank's lawyer, emphasized, "Keep in mind this is a drive-through we're talking about." As I see it, the only way this regulation makes sense is if it's a police entrapment scheme to arrest blind drivers.

The Occupational Safety and Health Administration (OSHA) fined a Boise, Idaho, plumbing company $7,875. When company workers rescued a fellow worker, they didn't shore up the collapsed trench or don hard hats before pulling him to safety. OSHA was forced to rescind the fine in the face of public outrage.

The Equal Employment Opportunity Commission (EEOC) ordered the Chicago-based Daniel Lamp Company to pay $123,000 in back pay to black workers who applied for jobs but were not hired. Located in a predominantly Hispanic neighborhood, the company employed twenty-one Hispanics and five blacks. The EEOC maintained that, given the area's population mix, the company should have employed 8.45 black workers.

Thousands of regulations mandate how we conduct virtually every aspect of our lives. The Code of Federal Regulations totals 131,803 pages, while the Federal Register listing proposed regulations totals 69,688 pages. With the full implementation of the Americans with Disabilities (1990), Nutrition Labeling and Education (1990), Civil Rights Restoration (1991), and the Clean Air (1990) Acts, there'll be thousands of additional pages of regulations.

You say, "There you go again, Williams, carrying water for businesses and not caring about little people." Let's look at it. Conservative estimates put regulatory compliance costs at about $1 trillion a year. Here's the question for you: If regulation raises the cost of business, who pays that cost? If you said ultimately consumers, you're half right. It's workers as well. As a result of regulations, jobs that would exist do not. If Washington makes it costly to get into business or expand an existing one, it is natural to expect less of either. This is one of the reasons this economic recovery is the puniest, in terms of job creation, since World War II. Because of regulations, it's cheaper for many companies that wish to increase output to pay worker overtime and have part-timers rather than hire full-time employees.

Any catastrophe attracts vultures to feed off carcasses. In the case of regulations, it's consultants, lawyers, and accountants. Businessmen know about business, but they know little about all the government mandates that can destroy their business. In come the vultures to advise and counsel them to the tune of thousands of dollars a day. Again, who pays? And again, it's consumers and workers.

Republicans should take a hard look at Washington's regulatory apparatus. One criterion for abolishing regulatory laws is to ask first whether they are constitutional: do they violate the Tenth Amendment? The second is a cost-benefit analysis to see whether the regulatory benefit equals the real-world cost. If Republicans don't help us, then we should do just as the founders did in response to King George's edicts— disobey them. "Williams," you say, "are you advocating disregard of these laws?" Yes, I am. There is no moral obligation for any of us to obey immoral or unconstitutional laws. But if you're caught, be prepared to pay the price.

EDUCATION

In 1983, the President's Commission on Excellence in Education gave us its report "A Nation at Risk," which warned us of the severe short-falls in our educational system. As a result the nation increased its financial commitment to schools. In 1991, the nation spent $413.8 billion on education, with about $248.6 billion of that amount going to primary and secondary schools. That averages just under $6,000 a pupil in total educational expenditures, an increase of nearly $3,000 a pupil during the past ten years. In kindergarten through twelfth grade, we average $3,846 a student. This compares with Japan's $2,200, Germany's $2,168, France's $2,221, and the United Kingdom's $2,768. Despite increased spending, national verbal SAT scores fell to an all-time low of 422 (44 points below its 1967 high of 466). Math SAT scores averaged 474 (18 points lower than its 1967 high of 492).

Despite the calls for more money for education, there is no evidence showing a strong positive relationship between educational expenditures and educational achievement. In fact there is a strong case for a negative correlation between educational achievement and expenditures. Iowa, Arizona, and Utah's per pupil educational expenditures are, respectively, $4,344, $3,276, and $2,629. Iowa's average combined SAT score totals 1,093, Arizona's is 1,005, and Utah's is 1,031. At the other extreme, New York spends $7,647 a pupil, New Jersey spends $7,795, and Washington, D.C., spends $7,550. Yet their student SAT averages are, respectively, 881, 885, and 840.

The academic achievement of American students in general is nothing to write home about; however, that received by most black students *is no less than criminal fraud. In many places, black students might have a high school degree in hand but not be able to function at the seventh- or eighth-grade level in math, science, and language.*

One cannot blame all our education problems on the education establishment, for there's enough blame for all participants to have their fair share. There are students who are alien, if not hostile, to the education process. There are parents who take little interest in their children's education, sometimes so much so that they don't require their youngsters to do homework, get adequate rest, and obey teachers. Of course, there are some teachers who have not mastered high school math and communication skills themselves. Administrators knowingly sanction the fraudulent practice of granting diplomas attesting that the student has mastered twelfth-grade skills when in fact the student might not have mastered even seventh- and eighth-grade skills.

Part of the problem is the stifling education monopoly. Another part is that schools are doing things that are in no way related to their mission. Under the guise of sex education youngsters are taught that premarital heterosexual and homosexual activity is OK so long as one takes adequate health measures. To reinforce this, some schools issue condoms to students without the knowledge or consent of parents and sometimes contrary to the expressed wishes of parents. Some schools provide birth control and abortion counseling for teen girls. Then there's what the educationists call "values clarification," where students are taught that there are no moral absolutes and no right and wrong forms of behavior—in a word many schools undermine values taught in the home.

The columns that follow address these and other issues involving education, concluding that the only long-run solution to the country's massive problems is to introduce competition into the system through educational vouchers or tuition tax credits. Both methods would help; however, I find tuition tax credits preferable because they are simpler and there is less chance of government control through the establishment of a Department of Vouchers.

Government Education Rip-Off

SEPTEMBER 2, 1992

Public school bells have chimed in a new semester, except for schools shut down by the National Education Association (NEA) or the American Federation of Teachers (AFT). Will our children receive a better education this year than last? It's doubtful. According to a March 1991 test, given in twenty countries by the Second International Assessment of Educational Progress, our nine- and thirteen-year-olds finished third from the bottom in science and second to the last in math.

As reported in Howard L. Hurwitz's new book, *The Best of Hurwitz on Education*, Albert Shanker, president of the AFT, lamented, "According to these exams, we're about on level with Spain and somewhat below Slovenia." Shanker's lament has a hollow ring, for it is he who said, as reported in the *Congressional Record*, August 1985, "When schoolchildren start paying union dues, that's when I'll start representing the interests of schoolchildren."

Keith Geiger, NEA president, said, "I'm encouraged by the growing acknowledgment that improving schools will cost money." Does better education require more tax gouging of the citizen? Here's a quiz for you, and no fair looking beyond the next two sentences. Iowa's students rank number one among the states on the SAT, and Washington, D.C., students rank number fifty. Which jurisdiction spends more per student? Believing what education hustlers tell us—more money means better education—I bet everyone picked Iowa. You're wrong. Iowa spends $4,344 per student, while Washington, D.C., spends $7,550.

New Jersey ($7,795), New York ($7,647), and Washington are the top three education spenders, yet their students' SAT scores, respectively, rank thirty-ninth, forty-second, and fiftieth. Indeed, when schools are ranked by spending and academic performance, the general pattern that emerges is the higher the expenditures, the lower the student SAT scores and vice versa.

Maybe the reason our kids do poorly on standardized tests is they are not asked questions about what they learn in school nowadays. They're given lessons on death and dying. In elementary school, they learn that having two mommies or two daddies is OK. Sex education classes begin in elementary school and continue through junior high and high school. It doesn't take years to master putting on a condom. What does take time is the assault on family values that takes place in bait-and-switch sex education classes.

Today's philosophy is that society, not individuals, is responsible for antisocial behavior. As a result of this harebrained philosophy, schools are not safe places. In New York City, there are thousands of kids kept in school who have been found guilty of serious misbehavior. Each day at least one New York schoolteacher requires hospital treatment. In Washington, D.C., some principals even wear bulletproof vests to school.

The education that most kids receive is nothing to write home about; however, that received by black youngsters is criminal. Black politicians, civil rights leaders, and other assorted liberals actively work against almost every attempt for effective reform such as tuition tax credits, vouchers or parental choice. But these two-faced antireform rascals want choice for themselves. That's why, for example, 46 percent of white—and 54 percent of black—Chicago public schoolteachers have their own children in private schools. Under the leadership of the American Civil Liberties Union and the National Organization for Women, liberals thwarted Detroit black parents' efforts to establish an all-male school.

The corrupting influence of the public education establishment must be challenged. We, particularly black people, are looking at the very likely prospect of a large portion of our youngsters being absolutely useless in the high-tech world of the twenty-first century.

Elite Campus Nazis

FEBRUARY 17, 1992

University of Cincinnati provost David Hartleb hired Edwin J. Nichols, a sensitivity trainer from Washington, D.C. During his faculty training session, Nichols tore into a young lady who had been at the university all of three weeks and who had earned a B.A. from Wellesley and graduate degrees from Harvard and New York University. The young lady was made to stand before an audience, which included one hundred or so faculty, while Nichols proceeded to berate her, saying, "This is a member of the privileged white elite." The young lady fell into tears in response to Nichols's continuous taunts. Not a single person rose to defend the lady. Afterward, Provost Hartlieb praised Nichols as perhaps the best sensitivity expert in America, saying his presence demonstrated the university's commitment to racial sensitivity.

Gestapo tactics and thought control are not confined to leftist government universities. At Dallas Baptist University, Professor David Ayers, arguing against contemporary feminist dogma, presented evidence that some of the differences between men and women originate in biology and genetics. Intimidated by campus feminists, the administration leveled a list of charges against Ayers and ordered Dean John Jeffrey to investigate. Jeffrey refused, saying that Ayers was engaged in legitimate scholarly research and that his rights to due process were being infringed. The university fired both men. As Lynne Cheney, former chairman of the National Endowment for the Humanities, says in *Telling the Truth*, feminists accuse those who challenge feminist dogma of antifeminist harassment. Charges of sexual harassment are often nothing more than right-wing smear tactics similar to those of the McCarthy era, where simply the charge of being a communist was enough to destroy careers.

In the *Harvard Educational Review*, a University of Wisconsin faculty member says professors should be open about their intention to "appropriate public resources to further progressive political agendas." This professor gives students three units of academic credit toward graduation for interrupting "business as usual in public spaces of library mall and administrative offices." A Princeton University professor says, "I teach in the Ivy League in order to have direct access to the minds of children of the ruling class." At Oberlin College, a student wrote an article in the campus newspaper critical of bias in his philosophy class. The professor left the classroom so other students could verbally abuse the dissenter. University of Hawaii professor Mari Matsuda argues that free speech deserves only "selective protection." Duke University's Stanley Fish writes, "The First Amendment is the first refuge of scoundrels."

Yale University president Benno Schmidt warned, "The most serious problems of freedom of expression in our society today exist on our campuses." On college campuses, there's the equivalent of the Nazi brownshirt thought-control movement. These brownshirts must laugh at us while we're taxed to finance their tyranny. They must chuckle at foolish businessmen, charitable foundations, and alumni associations who donate billions of dollars to colleges. Presidents, deans, and boards of trustees, who receive the money, have cowardly caved in to the demands of campus barbarians. Whenever taxpayers hear of these despicable campus tactics, they should pressure legislators to cut funding. Private contributors should summarily withhold donations until the solution is remedied. Nothing opens the arrogant closed minds of college administrators better than the sound of a pocketbook snapping shut.

A Hidden Success Story

MAY 19, 1993

Dr. Amyin Parker founded the Marcus Garvey School in South Central Los Angeles in 1975. If you visited, you'd see two-year-olds reciting the ABCs, three-year-olds counting in English, Spanish, and Swahili, and four-year-olds doing math. Down the hall, in Brenda Spencer's English class, you'd hear second graders spelling words like *pharmaceutical*, *entrepreneur*, and *cerebellum*. And if that surprises you, the same kids might recite Abraham Lincoln's Gettysburg address from memory and do elementary algebra. Or you could listen in on Vanessa Beverly's fourth-grade class, where the kids learn the periodic table, and hear a kid, without the blink of an eye, proudly state that "the chemical name for magnesium is Mg, and its atomic number is 12." Farther down the hall, you'd see Alfonso Thrower teaching math, including elementary differential calculus, to fifth and sixth graders.

Marcus Garvey is not a rich white suburban school. It's a black school with four hundred students located at 2916 W. Slauson Avenue, in a troubled section of Los Angeles. Its students are not gifted. They are ordinary kids, with concerned parents, going to an extraordinary school with black administrators and teachers who have unbounded pride and a sense of mission. What about costs? Marcus Garvey's tuition is $328 a month (about $3,200 a year). "How about the teachers?" you ask. "They must be real experts." I've got news for you. All have degrees, but none have teacher credentials. That tells us something. What they have going for them, according to Spencer, is freedom, freedom from bureaucratic controls and the right to tailor their program to a child's particular needs and abilities.

Marcus Garvey is such an educational oasis that if it had space and resources it could satisfy its waiting list of over two hundred students. Many ordinary black parents are willing to make great sacrifices to save their children from government school destruction. Interviewed by CNN's Robert Vito, parent Tony Jones said he drives his kid in from Riverside, California, each day just to attend Marcus Garvey—that's 120 miles round-trip.

Although we applaud Marcus Garvey's achievement, its sadder message is that the day-to-day destruction of black kids by government schools is absolutely unnecessary. They're destroyed in order to serve the empire-building needs of the government education establishment. I'm wondering when black people are going to wise up and ask: How long shall we sacrifice our children in the name of saving government schools and keeping the education establishment fat and happy? The solution is relatively simple: Empower parents.

What's needed is a tuition tax credit or voucher system. A tuition tax credit would work like this: Parents sending their kid to a nongovernment school would be allowed a deduction of $2,500 from their taxes. If a parent had no income, and owed no taxes, the state would send out a $2,500 check. A voucher system is something like food stamps. The state would issue educational vouchers. According to the Joint Center for Political and Economic Studies, 88 percent of black parents favor these educational choice plans.

If such a plan were implemented, we'd find many more schools like Marcus Garvey, Westside Preparatory, Ivy Leaf, A. Philip Randolph, and scores of other black-owned and -controlled schools doing an excellent job with meager resources. The reason we don't have educational choice is directly related to the awesome political power of the education establishment and unions seeking to avoid accountability. And black civil rights organizations come down on the side of the educational establishment and its unions.

School Choice

October 11, 1993

The hot issue on California's November ballot is Proposition 174, the "Parental Choice in Education Initiative." Voter approval would mean that parents who send their kids to nonpublic schools would receive a scholarship of $2,600 toward the costs of doing so. It would reduce the double burden of having to pay school taxes plus private school tuition. By the way, $2,600 is half the cost of California's public schools. The public education establishment is up in arms. According to David Harmer, author of *School Choice* (Northwest Publishers), upward of $10 million will be spent to campaign against Proposition 174.

Among the education establishment's many ruses for opposition to school choice are that choice will destroy public schools; that parents, particularly poor ones, are incapable of making wise choices; that if there is choice, private schools would "skim" off the best students, leaving public schools with the least motivated students and the least caring parents; that school choice will lead to school segregation by race; and that, even that if school choice is a good idea, there are not enough nonpublic schools.

Let's look at these arguments. The charge that choice will destroy public schools boils down to confessing that public schools are so rotten that, if given a choice, parents would opt out. Saying that parents can't make wise choices is another example of the education establishment's demeaning and paternalistic attitude. Even the most ill-informed parent could not do as much educational harm as many public schools now do. How about private schools "skimming" off students with caring parents? That objection to school choice amounts to callous arrogance and cruelty. It says that parents who want a better education and a brighter future for their children must be held hostage until some indefinite period in the future when public schools have improved. Public schoolteachers themselves don't wait; they enroll their own children in nonpublic schools at a rate higher than everybody else. How about the racial segregation argument? Surveys report that up to 88 percent of blacks favor school choice; plus, nonpublic schools are far more racially integrated than public schools. What about the "not enough private schools" argument? That reflects resolute ignorance of how markets work. In the 1970s, there were no video rental shops or computer software stores. Neither were there all the VCR and computer repairmen necessary. Should we have held up sales of computers and video machines until software and video rental shops were in place? Consumers owning computers and videos created the demand for software and video rental shops and repairmen. It'd be the same with private schools. Lots of parents with $2,600 scholarships would create the demand, and hence the supply, for private schools.

The education establishment's self-serving arguments against school choice have no merit whatsoever. In 1983, the National Commission on Excellence in Education said, "The educational foundations of our society are presently being eroded by a rising tide of mediocrity that threatens our very future as a nation and a people." Since then, we've poured additional billions into public education, and instead of improving student performance, the situation has gotten far worse.

The burden of proof lies with the education establishment to show how parents, acting through school choice programs, could possibly do more educational harm to their children than is being done now. And, by the way, school choice is not a threat to the many good teachers now working under the yoke of the education bureaucracy, unions, and the daily horrors of public schools. Choice offers them a way out— start their own private schools.

Yes, We Can

JANUARY 19, 1994

"I will not let you fail. Kids don't fail. Teachers fail. School systems fail. Colleges that turn out teachers who cannot teach fail." That was Marva Collins's attitude when she started Chicago's Westside Preparatory School on the second floor of her home in 1975 with $5,000. Since that time, the school has grown from six to two hundred and fifty students, with hundreds on the waiting list, and a worldwide reputation for excellence.

Last week, I had the pleasure of an on-site visit to the Marva Collins Preparatory School of Cincinnati (MCPSC) that's affiliated with the Chicago school. In 1990, Cleaster Mims started the school with twenty-four students in the basement of the Olivet Baptist Church. With volunteer help, Mims and her board of directors were able to purchase the Cincinnati Hebrew Day School building. There are now 126 students, with dozens on the waiting list.

Virtually all the MCPSC students are from low- and moderate-income households. All are black except two. Grades go from preschool through eighth. Almost 90 percent of the students score at grade level on standardized tests. Many score as high as two and a half, and some as high as six, grades above grade level. Boys come to school wearing a white shirt and tie, and girls wear jumpers and blouses. I visited every single class and saw students bristling with enthusiasm. In one class, sixth-, seventh- and eighth-grade students were at the blackboard writing solutions to a fairly high level of precalculus math problems.

That's just part of the story because you must be wondering what government agency gave Mims the grant money to start the school. There was, and is, none. Reverend Booth, pastor of the Olivet Baptist Church, recalls the school's financially shaky beginning: "Two or three mothers wouldn't give up. We started with a raffle." Plus, Mims and other good Cincinnatians, white and black, began fund-raising events and made charitable donations.

Now you say, "What's the tuition?" It's $3,000 a year for one kid and $4,000 for two. Tuition doesn't cover all operating costs, but here's what happens. Parents chip in their time and skills to build bookshelves, do repair work, and maintain an after-school center to help working parents. Then there's the energetic and persuasive Mims and her board of directors beating the bushes for used equipment and scholarship funds. Such zeal to provide black kids with a better education makes saying no to a request for financial help difficult—I know, firsthand.

There's a message in this story about Mims and her helpers. The message is that black people, even those with meager means, have the resources to solve problems meaningfully. That has always been the case until we were sold the idea that we are helpless victims of a racist society and that government programs, politicians, and assorted poverty pimps were our salvation.

For people who say they care about the destruction of black kids' future by government schools, I want them to answer some questions for me. What kind of racism and poverty stops us from having a raffle, if needed, to start a school? Do we really have worry about racial integration before there can be black educational excellence? How many more generations of black children's education are we going to allow to be destroyed as they're held hostage by an incompetent, costly, self-serving government education establishment? If you think we are helpless, you don't have half the character of a Cleaster Whitehurst-Mims.

Tidbits Update

FEBRUARY 16, 1994

Liberals fight tooth and nail against all efforts to enact school choice legislation, saying we must improve, not abandon, public schools. But according to a Heritage Foundation survey, 70 percent of the congressional Hispanic Caucus and 30 percent of the congressional Black Caucus members have their own children in private schools. These children rub shoulders with the children of other antichoice advocates such as President Clinton, Al Gore, and Jesse Jackson. Nationally, only 6 percent of Hispanic and 4 percent of black families have children in private schools. But they'd like to. According to a 1992 Gallup survey, 67 percent of Hispanic parents and 76 percent of black parents favor school choice. Some years ago, D.C. delegate Walter Fauntroy explained this seeming inconsistency between black leaders and their followers, saying that his children had only one life to live. Public schoolteachers feel the same way. They've abandoned public schools in droves—for their children.

Are you looking forward to Clinton's Canadian-style health care? Canadian citizens wait for weeks and months to get medical treatments you or I get in a day. But how about the Canadian elite? In Ottawa, there's a military hospital built to provide services for military personnel. But according to the Toronto *Globe and Mail* (1/29/94), the hospital maintains a Senior Executive Clinic whose primary patients are the "900 deputy ministers, assistant deputies, departmental directors and heads of special agencies." Canada's politicians found their way to the "no-wait" clinic as well, including "65 senators, 166 MPs [members of Parliament] and 198 senior executives." I guarantee that if our health care system is socialized, our politicians and bureaucrats will get the same special privileges while we wait in line and pick up the tab.

Here's an update on the quota front from the *Texas Republic* magazine (January–February 1994). The University of Texas Law School's principal criterion for admitting students is a composite number called the "Texas index" that combines the applicant's grade point average and admissions test score (LSAT). Whites are summarily denied admission with a score of 192 and below, and blacks and Hispanics, if their score is 179 or below. Blacks and Hispanics are summarily admitted with a score of 189 or higher, but whites must score 199 or higher. Thus, a Texas index score that brings acceptance letters to black and Hispanic applicants delivers rejection letters to whites.

The University of Texas Law School policy is not only offensive; it dishonors the great 1950 victory in *Sweatt v. Painter* where the U.S. Supreme Court ruled that the University of Texas Law School's refusal to admit blacks violated our Constitution's "equal protection" clause. As a practical matter, blacks and Hispanics ought to protest the school's 1990s version of its pre-1950 racist policy. Blacks and Hispanics who manage to do well and graduate have their law degrees cheapened. Law firms know about the process and discount their diplomas as affirmative action degrees. The fact that law schools feel as though they must "race-norm" admissions also says something about undergraduate education, namely, that twelve years of fraudulent primary and secondary education can't be repaired in four years.

But there's help on the way. The Washington, D.C.–based Center for Individual Rights has brought suit in the U.S. District Court in Austin on behalf of rejected white students, challenging the constitutionality of the University of Texas Law School's racist admission policy. As a supplement to the court challenge, private donors and foundations should withhold financial contributions to the school. Nothing opens the closed dogmatic minds of administrators better than the sound of a pocketbook snapping shut.

Back to School

AUGUST 24, 1994

I've been making regular visits to my doctor and taking his advice for twenty years and getting sicker and sicker while he's been charging me more and more. But I've got an appointment for more consultation next week. "You're crazy, Williams," you say. "You've got a quack doctor, but you're a fool to keep taking his advice!" We can say the same about Americans taking the advice of an education establishment that has brought us one educational disaster after another while going deeper and deeper into our pocketbooks. And now it's talking outcome-based education (OBE) and Goals 2000. Let's review its record.

American students rank last on most international comparisons of academic achievement. Today's achievement test scores are lower than they were in 1960. Colleges expend huge resources on high school math and English remedial courses. About a third of major corporations are teaching employees reading, writing, and math. Twenty-six percent of our students are in special education classes, compared to 1 percent and 2 percent in other developed nations. Instead of concentrating on core academic subjects, our students spend a large chunk of the school day on subjects like the environment, AIDS, multiculturalism, consumer affairs, and sex education.

When I was a kid, school disciplinary problems consisted of chewing gum in class, passing notes, running in hallways, and an occasional after-school fist fight. That's changed. The U.S. Justice Department reports as many as 500,000 violent incidents a month in the nation's public secondary schools. Each month, 1,000 teachers require medical attention because of in-school assaults; 125,000 are threatened. Being fifty-eight years old, I find this incredible. When I was in school, despite attending school in the slums of North Philadelphia, no kid would have dreamed of threatening, much less assaulting, a teacher.

Thomas Sowell, a senior research fellow at the Hoover Institution, sheds light on what's wrong in his recent book *Inside American Education*. Education majors achieve much lower SAT scores than those choosing other majors. When they finish college, it's the same story. Education majors are outscored on the Graduate Record Exam by other majors anywhere from 91 to 259 points. College students who major in education are among the least qualified. Some of the least-qualified students, taught by the least qualified-professors, have been entrusted with the education of our children. We shouldn't be surprised by their falling for fads and substituting methods that work for methods that sound good. This mediocrity isn't new. When Harvard University's president retired in 1933, he told the trustees that Harvard's Graduate School of Education was a "kitten that ought to be drowned." More recently, a knowledgeable academic said, "The educationists have set the lowest standards and require the least amount of hard work." In some circles, education departments have become known as the university's "intellectual slums."

It's difficult to get rid of grossly incompetent teachers. During a hearing to dismiss an incompetent English teacher, she was given a ten-word vocabulary test. She could neither pronounce nor define the word "agrarian." She could pronounce "suffrage" but defined it as "people suffering from some reason or other." She defined "ratify" as "to get rid of something." The judge ordered her reinstated.

More money isn't the solution. More money will just deliver more expensive incompetents. We must look to broader application of private and public school choice experiments going on across the nation. Plus, we must give greater support to dedicated public schoolteachers and principals bucking edicts from politicians, boards of education, and teacher unions in an attempt to educate our kids.

Destroying Our Children

October 19, 1994

According to the National Right to Read Foundation, last year the National Adult Literacy Survey reported that among adults with twelve years of schooling, more than 96 percent couldn't read, write, or compute well enough to attend college. In 1990, 40 million young Americans with nine to twelve years of schooling could not make sense out of a printed page. Only 56 percent of blacks over the age of fourteen could read.

There's little new about this downward spiral. In 1964, 20 percent of Selective Service registrants scored in the lowest rank (Category V) on the Armed Forces Qualifications Test (AFQT), making them noninductible; another 20 percent scored a little better, thus putting them in Category IV.

How do liberals and the civil rights, and education establishments explain these results? If you said a heritage of slavery, racism, poverty, a need for an outcome-based education program, and not enough education money, go to the head of the class. We've been duped. Let's look at it, but first, a bit of history.

During World War II, only 9 percent of recruits scored in Category V on the AFQT. Most of these were Depression-era young men who never attended school. In 1930, only 3 million older Americans couldn't read, compared with today's 40 million. Also, in 1930, 80 percent of blacks could read, compared to only 56 percent today. If we buy the liberals' excuses for today's educational mess, we must also believe that there was less racism and poverty and more spent on education in 1930 than today.

That's nonsense. The explanation for what we see today is that we've allowed hustlers, quacks, and charlatans to sell us on harebrained schemes that could work nowhere, nohow. One of these schemes is that there are five million students in special education classes with four million of them having no physical or mental handicap—unless it's that new handicap called attention deficit disorder. By the way, when teachers sent notes home about my not paying attention in class, Mom cured it overnight.

How do liberals and the education establishment respond to efforts to reverse the educational destruction of our kids? They attack. A case in point is Thaddeus Lott, the principal of Houston's Mabel B. Wesley Elementary School. Nearly all his students are poor and black. Yet, on standardized tests, they average at least one year above grade level. According to a story in *Destiny* magazine (October 1994), Wesley Elementary consistently produces test scorers in the top 80 to 90 percent of the Houston Independent School District (HISD), which includes Houston's wealthy areas. The HISD's early response to Lott's success was to deny Wesley Elementary materials given to other schools. HISD representatives barged into a first-grade teacher's class, accused her of cheating to raise student scores, and barred her from the class while they conducted a search. Of course, they found nothing. Now, as a result of parental demands and publicity, Lott's methods have been exported to other Houston public schools.

Lott's success is driven by his simple educational creed: "Students, given opportunity and direction, can learn. Blacks and other minorities are the intellectual match of white children." The trouble for Lott is that the education establishment sees him as an authoritarian, anti-modern principal who uses phonics, rote, and drill to teach students.

I say great—we need more Lotts. Black people must stop allowing muddleheaded liberals, civil rights organizations, and a self-serving education establishment to make our children virtually useless for the high-tech world of the twenty-first century. And, by the way, white education is nothing to write home about either.

THE ENVIRONMENT & HEALTH

Concern for the environment is legitimate. We must find ways to make individuals responsible for the pollution costs they impose on others. However, much of what is called environmentalism is motivated by nothing more than a power grab—a desire for centralized planning. Because socialism is well on its way toward the dustbin of history, renaming it is the only way to resurrect its respectability. That new name, as a means to gain public support and sympathy for central planning and control, is environmentalism.

Just as the communists did to dupe the public, environmentalists must also promote the big lie. In the case of environmentalists, it is what mankind's productive activity is doing to the earth. In the early 1970s environmental groups were warning us that mankind's productive activity was leading to global cooling and that the snow belt would reach as far south as Mexico by the next century. During the 1980s, they switched their tune, and, using the identical weather and geologic data, they warned of global warming, telling us that polar ice caps would melt and flood the low-lying coastal areas of the world. All the environmentalists' most dire warnings have been routinely dismissed by scientifically respected geologists and climatologists. Columns in this section reveal some aspects of the environmentalist agenda.

The liveliest single policy issue during President Clinton's first two years in office was national health care. The Clinton administration, in the name of correcting some of our health care problems, supported measures that would have nationalized up to one-seventh of our soci-

ety. Clearly, as the public agreed in handing him an embarrassing defeat, there are health care problems. But they do not warrant the potential destruction of a health system that provides the best services available in the world.

The columns in this section discuss many of the issues surrounding health care. Canada's single-payer system, held up as a model for the United States, is exposed. Not much sophistication is needed to conclude that ours is superior. Just observe what people do. Far more Canadians, and for that matter other foreigners, seek medical services from U.S. hospitals than U.S. citizens seek services at Canadian hospitals.

Animal Rights Lunatics

MARCH 12, 1990

First, let's get down to the numbers. In the United States alone, there are 100 million cows, 10 million sheep, 53 million pigs, 5.5 billion chickens, and, excluding those in Congress, 259 million turkeys. For the most part, while not treated as humans, these cute animals are well fed and well cared for, and their owners make great efforts to ensure that they're fruitful and multiply.

Let's imagine the realization of the animal rights activists' dream, wherein Congress enacts an emancipation proclamation granting a bill of rights to our feathery, leathery, and furry friends; what do you think will happen to their care and population size? I can just see a cow, with an emaciated face and a forlorn look in her eyes, asking her former master, "How come you don't feed and care for me anymore? You used to protect me and my children from kidnapping [rustling], but now you don't give a hoot." "Right on! Right on!" say the sheep, chickens, turkeys, and pigs.

It doesn't take too much imagination to guess the former master's reply. He says, "When you were my property, I was rewarded for making sure you were well fed and protected; now that you're free, there's nothing in it for me, so tough it out as best you can."

"There you go again, Williams," you say, "promoting that selfish,

'What's in it for me?' attitude." I plead guilty to the charge, but I ask, When was the last time you went out of your way to feed or nurse a sick cow or pig?

Let's forget about cows and pigs, think about elephants; after all, an elephant is an animal. There is an increasingly vocal call for a worldwide ban on ivory sales in the name of saving the African elephant from extinction. Will this improve the elephant's chances for survival? Not according to two researchers for the Institute of Political Economy at Utah State University, Randy T. Simmons and Urs P. Kreutner, in their article, "Herd Mentality" (Policy Review, fall 1989). In Kenya, where ivory sales are banned, the elephant population has fallen from sixty-five thousand to nineteen thousand over the past decade. In Kenya, elephants are not viewed as valuable economic resources, except as a boost to tourism. Poachers succeed in illegally killing them because few people have any economic incentive to protect them.

On the other hand, in Zimbabwe, where ivory sales are legal, the elephant population has grown from thirty thousand to forty-three thousand over the last decade. In Zimbabwe, elephants have an economic value—about $5 million to twenty-four tribal villages. As a result, villagers protect elephants from poachers, cull the herds to prevent starvation that comes from overpopulation, and jealously guard their investment in future ivory production.

Other examples of these patterns prevail throughout Africa. The bottom line is simple. When foreigners buy ivory products, they increase the economic value of the elephant herds, which, in turn, give African villagers greater incentive to care for and protect them.

There's nothing novel or puzzling about the relationship between ownership, economic value, and care. Imagine that the animal rights lunatics got a law passed banning the sale of beef in the name of saving cows; you can bet the rent money that our cattle population would fall dramatically.

People who are serious about the long-term survival of elephants, rhino, minks, and other cuties should call for private ownership, buy plenty of the products made from these animals, and smuggle if necessary. The New York City fringe of the animal rights movement, who intimidate and throw red paint on women wearing minks, will increase their own survival chances if they avoid doing the same to my wife when she sports her mink coat.

Madness in the Air

JUNE 13, 1990

I don't know about you, but environmentalists, conservationists, and animal rights loonies are getting on my nerves. What's worse, the White House and Congress are paying attention to them. You say, "OK, Williams, what's the beef? What do you have against these wonderful earth and animal huggers? They just want to make things right."

Ingrid Newkirk, director of People for Ethical Treatment of Animals (PETA), intones, "The smallest form of life, even an ant or a clam, is equal to a human being." Thus the justification to harass, threaten, burglarize, and destroy medical research facilities. It's also the justification to trivialize human tragedy. Newkirk advises, "Six million Jews died in concentration camps, but six billion broiler chickens will die this year in slaughterhouses." This vision is also the excuse to torch fur stores and spray paint women wearing fur coats. The animal rights people don't impress me with this kind of cowardly terrorism. I'd be more impressed on hearing news of their spray painting and slashing animal skins worn by the Hell's Angels.

Animals are not equal to humans. If animals have any human trait, it's racism. Don't believe me? Just watch a cat walk by a dog. The dog terrorizes the cat solely because it's a cat. But don't feel sorry for cats, they act racist too. Just let a mouse walk by a cat and see what happens. I wonder whether animal rights people support animal racism.

Environment/conservation loonies get Congress to do things that kill us. The use of asbestos has been banned even though it poses very little health risk. The Environmental Protection Agency (EPA) orders its removal at a cost of $9 billion a year even though its removal is a greater health hazard. According to columnist Warren Brookes, Congress's listening to asbestos loonies caused the *Challenger* disaster. NASA and Thiokol used to use an asbestos-based putty to seal rocket O-rings. Fearing lawsuits, they stopped. In the first twelve flights after the asbestos putty ban, there were four occurrences of O-ring erosion. Malcolm Ross of the U.S. Geological Survey said, "There is no doubt in my mind that the *Challenger* disaster was caused by the EPA's asbestos paranoia."

Aflatoxin, a soil fungus that affects grains, is a known cancer-causing agent that had been effectively treated through the use of the fumigant ethyl dibromide (EDB). The environmental loonies got Congress to ban the use of EDB. Now much of our grain is suspected of being contaminated with dangerous levels of aflatoxin. The ban on EDB puts consumers at a thousand times greater health risk. EDB is reported to be only one half as carcinogenic as the chloroform levels in most tap water.

The asbestos and EDB stories were easily found by Warren Brookes. But I bet you never heard about it in the news media sympathetic to the environmental/conservationist loonies.

The loonies have us going and coming. Twenty years ago, environmentalists were clucking that the earth was cooling and a new ice age was coming unless Congress did something about it. How do you like that for arrogance? Congress is supposed to be so powerful that it can stop the onset of an ice age. The same environmentalists are now clucking about global warming. That hole in the ozone layer, up north, opens and closes naturally as a result of changes in the earth's magnetic fields. If anything is going to cause global warming, it's the hot air coming from Congress. The bottom line is that Americans are being suckered into a lower standard of living, fewer freedoms, and poorer health by a Congress that is in cahoots with environmental/conservationists loonies. Some of these people even hail AIDS because they see it as a way to relieve the earth's population pressures. Isn't that disgraceful?

Victimized by Liberals

AUGUST 29, 1990

The liberals, their fellow travelers in the conservationist and environmental movements, and a short-sighted, immoral Congress have messed up our country. The Middle East crisis is an early warning of things to come. Let's face it; we've put men, planes, ships, and tanks in the Middle East for one reason: to protect our access to oil. Anyone who says we're there to make the area safe for democracy is whistlin' "Dixie." The dominant feature of the Middle East is the contempt the people there hold for democratic principles, human life, and liberty.

Many people say we don't have an energy policy, but that's not true. We have a policy, but it borders on insanity. Let's look at it. Point Arguello oil field, off the California coast, has been ready for two years and could add as much as 4.2 million gallons a day to our domestic oil supply. It could be on-line in just six months. However, the California liberals, with the help of state officials, have shut it down.

According to conservative estimates by the American Petroleum Institute, accelerated leasing of the outer continental shelf oil fields could yield 32 million gallons/day; leasing and developing the Arctic National Wildlife Range would yield 20 million gallons/day; onshore Alaska leasing would yield 27 million gallons/day; and onshore leasing in other states would yield about 5 million gallons/day. These facts lead me to the conclusion that, if we have to land troops to ensure access to oil, they would be better deployed in Washington.

Several countries generate most of their electrical power from nuclear energy. In France, nuclear plants generate 68 percent of their electricity. Americans invented nuclear energy, yet it accounts for only 18 percent of our electrical power. It takes us more than ten years to build a nuclear power plant because of costly litigation and regulation. In Japan and France, the process start to finish is slightly over six years. Moreover, theirs are built at approximately half of what it costs us. You say, "Oh, that's because their plants are less safe." Nonsense, French plants are built to U.S. specifications under license from Westinghouse.

Liberals demonstrating all over the country have hamstrung our nuclear power industry. With media complicity, they claim nuclear energy is unsafe, but they can't point to a single U.S. citizen who has died as a result. Doing the bidding of the environmental crowd, Congress sabotages our nuclear development. As a result scores of people die each year from coal mine accidents, black lung disease, and air pollution from power generation by coal.

Americans may be able to weather the high prices of oil, but the real liberal-generated disaster is in the not-too-distant future. Several Third World countries, including Iraq, are developing intercontinental missiles. If Iraq had those missiles now, Saddam Hussein might very well target New York, Washington, or Los Angeles in response to any U.S. military action against him. Sure we'd wipe him off the face of the earth, but possibly millions of Americans would have died from lethal chemical or biological agents.

Deploying and developing a strategic defense system would enable us to address that threat, not to mention the threat of an accidental or ethnic terrorist launch from the Soviet Union. But the liberals in and out of Congress have gutted the program. They see tax dollars used for handouts as a better bargain. I hope the day never comes when millions of Americans die from chemical or bacteriological agents. But if it does, I hope we remember that today's Congress had a big hand in it.

The Environmental Protection Agency and the Radon Lie

April 29, 1992

The Environmental Protection Agency (EPA) has emerged as one of the most evil organizations in our country, and that's the plan. EPA bureaucrats, according to at least one spokesman, long for the day when a call from the EPA will instill as much citizen fear as a call from the Internal Revenue Service. Lies, propaganda, and fear-mongering are crucial elements to their agenda. Philip H. Abelson, the science adviser to the American Association for the Advancement of Science, exposes the radon phase of the EPA agenda.

Writing in *Regulation* (fall 1991), a publication of the Washington-based CATO Institute, Abelson warns that Congress and the EPA are going to force us to pay billions of dollars for radon control measures for negligible health benefits. Central to the EPA's power agenda are official lies like "43,000 people per year die of lung cancer attributable to radon." Abelson says that these numbers are not supported by epidemiological studies but extrapolated from old reports of the experiences of uranium miners, the vast majority of whom were smokers.

The EPA reports that five Midwest states have the highest levels of radon. Taken together, these states have twice the national average; however, the incidence of lung cancer in these states is only 80 percent of the national average. Colorado, North Dakota, and Iowa have the highest radon levels, and their lung cancer deaths average 41 per 100,000 of the population. However, Delaware, Louisiana, and California have the nation's lowest radon levels, but their average lung cancer death rate is 66 per 100,000.

A harebrained assumption underlying many EPA-mandated regulatory standards is that substances toxic at high levels are also injurious at low levels. We all know that one cause of stomach cancer is excessive ingestion of table salt. If the EPA and Congress found this out, they might legislate a total ban on table salt. Indeed, a number of elements that are absolutely essential to human life in small doses are carcinogenic at high doses.

EPA bureaucrats take the position that no level of radon is safe. If the EPA, along with environmental loonies and congressional supporters, has its way, homeowners are going to pay about a trillion dollars to bring their homes up to a zero radon standard. The benefit from this expenditure, for the overwhelming majority of the nation, will approximate zero.

As a part of its fear-mongering campaign, the EPA makes baseless claims such as "Children are three times as susceptible to radon as adults." In 1990, the EPA circulated a revision of its "Citizen's Guide." Reviewers labeled the document as "a clever example of deceptive advertisement and distortion of scientific fact," "improperly presented scientific information, omission and just plain fictitious statements," and "an advertisement for radon contractors." As a result of scathing criticism, the EPA's 1990 "Citizen's Guide" was not published.

The EPA is nearly 100 percent wrong about the dangers of radon, but the fact that it's wrong doesn't exempt you and me from the cost of its alarmist propaganda. Homeowners are increasingly finding that to sell their homes they must test for radon and, if necessary, make repairs. If the EPA has its wish that household radon levels not exceed those of outside air, almost every homeowner will be forced to make expensive household repairs.

Abelson suggests that the EPA abandon scare tactics and focus its efforts on identifying areas with unusually high radon levels. He also suggests an independent epidemiological study of the extent to which nonsmokers are affected by ambient radon. The EPA refuses to conduct such a study.

Econo-Eco Update

JUNE 24, 1992

We are misled, lied to, and deceived in so many ways that the average American doesn't know whether he's coming or going. So how about some econo-eco facts?

Is America running out of forests and trees, thereby creating the necessity for Congress to do something? Misled by the "watermelons" (those who are green outside but red inside), and their news media helpers, the average American would say yes. However, according to the American Forest Council, there are now more trees growing in America than seventy years ago, at least 230 billion in total, or about one thousand trees for each American man, woman, and child. So when the supermarket clerk asks, "Paper or plastic bag?" I'm going to say paper.

Congress and the media get their ecology advice from people like Earth First activist Judy Bari, who says, "I think if we don't overthrow capitalism, we don't have a chance of saving the world ecologically. I think it is possible to have an ecologically sound society under socialism. I don't think it is possible under capitalism." In all likelihood, Judy Bari has not seen the ecological disaster in the former Soviet republics. It's so bad that it is a misdemeanor to discard cigarettes in the Volga River because of the fire hazard.

How about your money? Out of each dollar, the amount the typical American family spends on food is eleven cents, on housing and household expenses sixteen cents, and taxes forty cents. Congressional tax gouging is the main reason family take-home income is under siege, forcing mothers into the workplace. Congress is not only destroying our country through debt and deficits but increasingly creating conditions where children have to be left alone or raised by day care providers. By the way, what's your guess: Will Congress tax gouge us more or less next year?

Are you pushing for Congress to give us a "wonderful" nationalized health care system like that of our northern neighbor? If you are, Canada's prestigious Fraser Institute (604-688-0221) has an update for you. Nearly 261,000 Canadians had to wait a bit for surgical and medical procedures. In Newfoundland, the average waiting time for heart surgery was forty-two weeks, but it was only ten weeks in New Brunswick. However, Newfoundland patients requiring ophthalmological procedures had a leg up, waiting only three weeks, while their Manitoba neighbors had to wait thirteen weeks. Throughout Canada, the average time spent in the surgical waiting line is thirteen weeks for plastic surgery, nine weeks for gynecology, sixteen weeks for orthopedics, and fourteen weeks for cardiology, and in no case is the average wait under three weeks. It's no wonder so many Canadians, particularly their elite bureaucrats, are showing up in hospitals in Buffalo, Rochester, Detroit, and other border cities. The bottom line is that if you like government housing, government schools, government hospitals, and government mail delivery, you're going to love nationalized (government) health care.

How about acid rain? The ten-year Environmental Protection Agency–sponsored National Acid Precipitation Assessment Program reports that the average Adirondack lake is no more acidic now than it was before the Industrial Revolution; only 35,000 of the 200 million acres of U.S. lakes are too acidic to support fisheries, and most of this acidity is natural. Indeed, as reported by the Dallas-based National Center for Policy Analysis, studies have shown that acid rain has improved crop yield in Sweden and fertilizes 300 million acres of eastern U.S. forest.

Just because Soviet communism is dead doesn't mean that we're safe; the new comrades, just as contemptuous of the principles of liberty and dedicated to its destruction, are the enviro-freaks and do-gooders.

Environmental Update

SEPTEMBER 9, 1992

Contrary to environmentalist nonsense, people are not the earth's worst enemy. According to *Science* magazine (November 1982), the world's termites generate more than twice the amount of carbon dioxide we generate by burning fossil fuels. The termite's digestive system is so efficient that it converts 90 percent of the wood eaten into carbon dioxide, methane, and other gases and then belches it into the atmosphere.

Then there are ants. According to an atmospheric chemist at Bell Laboratories and zoologists from Cornell University, ants belonging to the Formicinae family produce large quantities of formic acid, which makes a significant contribution to acid rain. The formic acid is released when the ants fight and communicate with one another and also when they die. As a result, ants put an estimated 600,000 metric tons of formic acid into the atmosphere annually, an amount equal to the combined contributions of automobiles, refuse combustion, and vegetation. What should Congress and the Environmental Protection Agency (EPA) do about termites and ants? How about a training program to get termites to eat grass instead of wood? Should we bury dead ants in leak-proof EPA-approved hazardous waste containers?

In one important sense, some might consider environmentalists to be mass killers. Before the development of DDT, 200 million persons were stricken annually with mosquito-borne malaria, and 2 million died. In Sri Lanka in 1948, for example, before the introduction of DDT, there were 2.8 million cases of malaria each year. By 1963, the number of cases had fallen to 17 a year and remained low until the late 1960s, when environmentalist attacks in the United States prompted Sri Lanka officials to suspend spraying DDT. By 1968, according to the *New American* (June 1992), the number of malaria cases in Sri Lanka had risen to 1 million, and, by 1969, 2.5 million Sri Lankans had become infected with malaria each year. According to the EPA's own 1972 report, DDT "is not a carcinogenic hazard to man. The uses of DDT under the registrations involved here do not have a deleterious effect on freshwater fish, estuarine organisms, wild birds or other wildlife."

Listening to environmental experts in 1987, Congress passed the Asbestos Hazard Emergency Response Act requiring asbestos removal in schools. According to the *New England Journal of Medicine* (June 1989) and *Science* (January 1990), undisturbed asbestos poses little risk for lung disease and the removal of asbestos causes significant increases in asbestos levels. In September 1990, the EPA finally admitted that asbestos removal can pose a severe health hazard. Now the question is, Will all those law-abiding people who spent billions of dollars obeying Congress's stupid, costly edict be compensated?

How about PCBs (polychlorinated biphenyls)? Because they are nonflammable and stable under extreme temperatures, they are ideal as lubricants and coolers for air conditioners, transformers, and other electrical equipment. According to a comprehensive 1981 report by the National Institute for Occupational Safety and Health, there were no statistically significant cancer effects on workers exposed to PCBs for twenty to forty years. But the EPA banned PCBs anyway, causing virtually all U.S. transformer stations to go back to mineral oil. One effect of the ban was the July 29, 1990, Chicago fourteen-square-mile blackout resulting from a fire in a malfunctioning transformer that damaged a generating plant. Rioting broke out during the blackout; three people died. This blackout, property damage, and loss of life would not have occurred if the incombustible PCB was in use.

And just think, we thought the demise of the Soviet Union meant the end to threats to our safety and liberty.

Should Congress Outlaw Thanksgiving?

OCTOBER 31, 1991

The optimal amount of anything harmful or bad is never zero. How about the reckless discard of used items—littering? Would you have had our Desert Storm troops pick up spent ammunition before moving to their next objective so as not to litter? What about zero air pollution and zero theft? To get that requires that we cease production and have guards everywhere. The optimal amount of anything harmful or bad is never zero simply because it is much too costly to achieve it.

"OK, Williams," you say, "but I draw the line at cancer-causing substances—zero carcinogens for me!" If that's your position, we'd better outlaw our traditional Thanksgiving dinner. The American Council on Science and Health (1995 Broadway, New York) has put out its "Holiday Dinner Menu" detailing the toxins and carcinogenic agents that garnish our Thanksgiving feast.

If you're serving cream of mushroom soup as a starter, be aware that it contains hydrazine, which is a known carcinogen. A side dish of radishes, cherry tomatoes, and celery contains glucosinolates (which causes antithyroid activity), nitrate (a carcinogen), and psoralems (a mutagen and a carcinogen).

If you're having turkey as the entrée, be careful. Turkey contains heterocyclic amines and malonaldehyde, two powerful mutagens. However, if you hold the stuffing, you can avoid carcinogens like benzo-(a)pyrene, ethyl carbamate, and safrole. And if you hold the cranberry sauce, you won't add eugenol to your troubles. You might want to reconsider serving that old American standard—the baked potato. Potatoes contain oxalic acid, which causes kidney stones, and chaconine, which inhibits nerve function. If all that weren't bad enough, potatoes also contain arsenic.

Your dessert menu is just as hazardous. Pumpkin pie contains myristicin and red wine has methylglyoxal; myristicin and methylglyoxal are carcinogens. If you have a few mixed nuts on the side, you're eating afatoxins, one of the most potent cancer-causing agents known. You say, "Heck, Williams, with that kind of news, I'm just going to have a glass of water." Watch out! Water contains nitrate, which is toxic to humans and can convert to nitrite and subsequently form cancer-causing nitrosamines.

Of course, you can enjoy your Thanksgiving dinner, and not fear cancer, if you chow down in moderation. The toxic dose of potatoes is one hundred pounds, that of spinach, ten pounds, and if you hold your turkey consumption to less than 3.8 tons, you won't have to worry about malonaldehyde.

The conclusion we should draw from the American Council on Science and Health's menu is that almost everything we consume contains toxins or carcinogens; however, it's the dosage that counts. The human body does a wonderful job of metabolizing or excreting small doses of toxins and carcinogens. Another conclusion is that we should eat a varied diet so that we don't saturate ourselves with a particular chemical. But an even more important conclusion, contrary to propaganda by health "experts," is that nature is not as friendly, and man-made is not as evil, as we're led to believe. The cancer risk of one mushroom is 167 times greater than the dietary intake of EPA-banned PCBs (polychlorinated biphenyls) and EDB (ethylene dibromide).

The human dietary intake of nature's toxins is at least ten thousand times higher than toxins consumed through the usage of man-made pesticides. We would starve to death trying to consume zero toxins and carcinogens. If we allow the food Nazis to dictate our diets, we are going to have poorer health rather than better health and, to boot, slimmer pocketbooks.

Have a happy Thanksgiving and eat, drink, and be merry, of course, all in moderation.

Paying a Lot for Nothing

MARCH 3, 1993

Some laws are not worth obeying. Why? Because either they make us poorer with no comparable offsetting benefit or they are immoral. Take Occupational Safety and Health Administration restrictions on worker exposure to asbestos or formaldehyde. The estimated number of deaths from worker exposure to asbestos are 6.7 per 100,000 and from formaldehyde, 0.1 per 100,000 of the exposed population. Taking into account regulatory costs, the asbestos regulations cost us $117 million per life saved and the formaldehyde restrictions, $94 billion per life saved. "There you go again, Williams," you say, "putting a dollar value on human life. If a law can save just one life isn't it worth it?" I say, If you think saving lives is important, irrespective of cost, think of the thousands of lives that could be saved by a law mandating a 5-mph speed limit. Would you vote for such a law? You say, "Williams, that's ridiculous!" What you really mean to say is, "That's too costly!"

The asbestos hoax, incidentally, was engineered by the environment-crazed portion of our population assisted by the multibillion-dollar-a-year asbestos removal industry. It's a hoax that led to the tragic deaths of the spaceship *Challenger* crew. According to Michael J. Bennett's "The Asbestos Racket," the Consumer Product Safety Commission's asbestos ban made the Fuller O'Brien Company discontinue the manufacture of standard O-ring putty that had been used successfully in other shuttles and rockets. The National Aeronautics and Space Administration (NASA) putty lacked the resiliency of the Fuller O'Brien product. As a result of the tremendous heat and gas pressure on launch, the NASA putty contracted when it should have expanded.

The asbestos panic started with the typical environmentalist strategy of statistical lying. Drs. Irving Selikoff and Marvin Schneiderman estimated that fifty-eight thousand to seventy-five thousand people a year died from asbestos-related cancer. As reward for fear mongering, Schneiderman was made scientific adviser for the Environmental Protection Agency (EPA). In a recent Fifth Circuit Court of Appeals case, the court threw out the asbestos ban because the EPA couldn't even prove thirteen asbestos deaths a year. Hundreds of billions of dollars later, as we discover the hoax, the EPA and Schneiderman confess, "We made an inappropriate estimate."

Environmental regulation is often a front for behind-the-scenes special interests. The 1970 Clean Air Act fixed sulfur emission standards for power utilities. Utility companies met these standards by using low-sulphur clean Western coal instead of high-sulfur East Coast coal. In 1977, the Eastern coal-mining industry and unions, led by Senator Byrd (D-W.Va.), successfully lobbied for amendments to the 1970 Clean Air Act. Utilities now must meet percentage reductions in sulphur emissions regardless of the original sulphur content of the coal. This all but mandates installing expensive smokestack scrubbers. Thus, it no longer makes a difference whether the industry uses clean or dirty coal. Environmental laws are used to fatten the pocketbooks of the Eastern coal-mining establishment at the expense of public utility users, Western miners, and cleaner air. Businessmen and unions use environmentalists as a means to higher profits and wages. Payoffs to environmental organizations are "charitable" donations.

It's a beautiful scam because environmentalists and businesses appear public spirited, and complainers like Williams get tagged with not caring about the environment. This public rip-off is what the environmentalists mean when they say that concern for the environment is good business. And they're right. But for the average person, it means higher prices, fewer jobs, unnecessary deaths, and, sometimes, dirtier air.

Expert Nonsense

NOVEMBER 10, 1993

I worry about how we give self-declared experts the right to ruin our pocketbooks and country. We enact costly regulations based on predictions about the weather fifty years from now when the weatherman often can't get the prediction straight about tomorrow's weather. Richard Lindzen, an MIT meteorology professor, says, "Many oceanographers and atmospheric scientists working on the climate share the view that the present global-warming hypothesis is largely a political issue without scientific basis." Politically motivated predictions, particularly by those feeding at the federal pork trough, aren't new. Let's look at it.

Texas A&M professors Maurice and Smithson document phony predictions in a Hoover Institution publication titled *The Doomsday Myth*. In 1891, the U.S. Geological Survey predicted that there was little or no chance of finding oil in Texas. It's a good thing Texans ignored those birdbrains. In 1926, the Federal Oil Conservation Board predicted that the United States had a seven-year supply of oil remaining. In 1939, the Interior Department said we'd be out of oil in less than two decades. Ten years later, the secretary of the interior predicted that the end to the U.S. oil supply was almost in sight.

It's not just oil. Here are a few headlines from the *New York Times* between 1900 and 1908: "The End of Lumber Supply," "Timber Famine Near, Says Roosevelt and National Forest Service," "Urges Laws to Save Trees, Forest Will Be Wiped Out in Ten Years at Present Rates, Whipple Says." The doomsayers got us worried about water, too. Here are a few title captions from national magazines during the 1970s and 1980s: "The Water Crisis; It's Almost Here," "What to Do When the Well Runs Dry," "Water: Will We Have Enough to Go Around?" "Water, Water, Running Out," "A Grim Future for the Water-Short West." Tell all that to Americans in Iowa, Kansas, and Missouri.

If elitist fear-mongering made us tremble for a bit and later laugh at ourselves for being taken in, it would be one thing. But fear-mongering is killing Americans and making us poorer in the process. "Hey, Williams," you say, "that's a heady charge; back yourself up!" Part of the justification for Clinton's initiative to get Congress to mandate greater auto fuel economy is to save oil. It will result in Detroit manufacturing lighter cars that are less crashworthy. According to research done by Robert Crandall of the American Enterprise Institute, previous mandates cost ten thousand additional highway deaths and twenty thousand additional injuries each year. We can call this congressional policy a blood-for-oil policy. During the 1970s, Congress used tax incentives and mandates to encourage people to heavily insulate homes, businesses, and offices in the name of saving energy. In turn, this created problems of indoor pollution. Now the Environmental Protection Agency and the Occupational Safety and Health Administration mandate costly controls when 70 percent of all indoor pollutants can be eliminated through ventilation—opening windows.

America's fear-mongers don't mean to kill us and make us sick. They do mean to increase their own power, influence, and control over us, not to mention getting into our pocketbooks. There's nothing much more appealing than the idea that there's a crisis and that we must set up a temporary government agency to save us. What's more, there is nothing more permanent than a temporary government agency to handle a crisis. In the eyes of all, with the exception of California's bureaucrats, its drought is over. How much do you want to bet its water emergency management agency has not been disbanded?

The best thing Americans can do with experts is to charge them for each word of advice and then ignore their advice.

Junk Science

AUGUST 4, 1993

Hitler said, "The broad mass of a nation . . . will more easily fall victim to a big lie than to a small one." That's the spirit behind the junk science of today that Congress uses to gain greater control over our lives.

What we're being told about AIDS is a good example of junk science. *Rethinking AIDS*, a publication of the San Francisco–based Group for the Scientific Reappraisal of the HIV/AIDS Hypothesis, points out

that female prostitutes often have two hundred to three hundred partners a year. You'd naturally assume that they would have much higher
exposure to HIV/AIDS than the vast majority of heterosexuals and contribute to an explosion of the disease. Paradoxically, according to the
March edition of *Rethinking AIDS*, no heterosexual epidemic has occurred and no evidence of female prostitutes transmitting HIV/AIDS
into the heterosexual community exists for any Western nation. Prominent researchers in the United States, Germany, Spain, Italy, and Britain conclude that the acquisition of HIV by men from female prostitutes is almost always drug-related.

The near absence of HIV among nondrug-using prostitutes is not
due to safer sex. Studies have reported that 5 to 50 percent of prostitutes were seropositive for syphilis and hepatitis B virus. Antibodies to
chlamydia, herpes, and gonorrhea were present in 95 to 100 percent.
Although politicians and the medical profession don't have the guts to
say it, much of the AIDS plague is a result of the drug-using, indiscrimi-
nate homosexual lifestyle sanctioned and advocated by liberals. If you
don't live that lifestyle, you run little risk of HIV/AIDS infection.

The bulk of junk science comes from the Environmental Protection
Agency (EPA). It puts out breathless lies such as kitchen appliances and
cellular telephones cause cancer. It's now investigating the possibility
that showers are linked to cancer because chemicals in tap water are
more fully released in the spray of a shower. Then there's the EPA-
sponsored hoax that secondhand, or passive, smoke is a class-A carcinogenic along with asbestos and benzene. The February 1993 edition
of the Washington-based *Complete* magazine reports that Yale University epidemiologist Alvan Feinstein, writing in the *Toxicological Pathology* journal, reported that he heard a prominent leader in epidemi-
ology support EPA's work on passive smoking, saying, "Yes, it's rotten
science, but it's a worthy cause. It will help us to get rid of cigarettes
and to become a smoke-free society." That's it in a nutshell: Scientific
lies are being used to control us.

Then there are "scientific" predictions. Paul Ehrlich, environmentalist guru and mentor to Vice President Al Gore, told Britain's Institute of Biology in 1969, "If I were a gambler, I would take even money
that England will not exist in the year 2000." And we thought British
prime minister John Major only had to worry about his economy.

Junk science has penetrated and captured some of our most prestigious institutions, like the National Academy of Sciences. Back in 1977, it warned of a new ice age. Its evidence was "Duration of the snow cover, animal migration, sea surface temperatures and microfossils on the ocean floor, not to mention declining average global temperatures." Now, it has switched tunes, telling us that the earth is warming.

Here's the plot as Senator Timothy Wirth (D-Colo.) confessed, as reported in Michael Fumenton's *Science under Siege*, "We've got to ride the global warming issue. Even if the theory of global warming is wrong, we'll be doing the right thing, in terms of economic policy and environmental policy."

The Environmental Protection Agency's Lies

JUNE 30, 1993

Let's face it. Tobacco smoke odor is offensive to some people. It causes allergic reactions and bronchial discomfort to others. Regardless of our personal tastes, we all should take note of the issues surrounding the recently announced tobacco industry lawsuit against the Environmental Protection Agency (EPA). The critical issue it raises is whether we should allow zealots to rig data and misuse science in their efforts to command and control others.

When the EPA classified environmental tobacco smoke (ETS) as a group-A carcinogen, putting it in the category with benzene and asbestos, its actions were based on statistical methodology that would earn an F for a sophomore statistics student, if not expulsion for intellectual dishonesty. Let's look at it.

Twenty-four of the thirty studies that the EPA reviewed reported no statistically significant ETS–lung cancer relationship. Of the eleven studies done by U.S. scientists, not one reported significant cancer risk. The EPA was aware of and ignored the findings of the two largest and most recent studies on ETS–lung cancer (Stockwell 1992; Brownson 1992, sponsored by the National Cancer Institute). Both studies report no increased lung cancer risk with exposure to ETS, as did 80 percent of the studies EPA had in its possession.

Biased and sloppy analysis like that would earn EPA officials an F, but here's what would lead to expulsion. All scientists require minimally what is statistically known as a "95 percent level of confidence" before they report a causal connection between two variables. In other words, they will accept a maximum level of 5 percent that the connection was by chance. In most cases, scientists want to make it tighter than that—a 99 or 98 percent level of confidence. But guess what the EPA did when it combined (and did so invalidly) several ETS–lung cancer studies? Unbeknownst and unreported to the public, it lowered the confidence interval to 90 percent! Had it stuck to the minimally acceptable practice of 95 percent, assignment of ETS as a group-A carcinogen would have been impossible. This is gross dishonesty, and all EPA bureaucrats involved should be summarily fired, including Carol Browner, who has come to their defense.

Let's say you hate the odor of tobacco smoke and smokers. That's OK. But the critical issue is whether you think it's good for our nation to allow government officials to deliberately misuse science. You might say, "So what! People shouldn't smoke anyway!" But when have you known liars to be satisfied with just one lie? The next lie could be about something you value that might be banned or restricted as a result.

You say, "But, Williams, tobacco smoke is offensive to me, and something needs to be done." I agree, and that's the benefit of private property. In your house, a person doesn't have the right to smoke without your permission. Why? Because it belongs to you. If you own a restaurant, bar, or office, it's the same thing. If I don't like your policy, I don't enter. It works the other way too. If a person owns a restaurant, bar, or office, and he permits smoking, you have the right to say you won't eat, drink, or work at his facility. As of late, Americans have abandoned this conflict-reducing role of private property in favor of government intimidation, threat, and violence. That's fine except when you consider that you may not always be on the side of the dominant coalition and that it will be you who is victimized by official lies, threats, and intimidation.

How Totalitarianism Works

MARCH 23, 1994

Philosopher David Hume said, "It is seldom that liberty of any kind is lost all at once." Let's apply this idea to our Second Amendment rights but start off talking about antismoking regulations.

The antismoking campaign started off attacking private property rights, with eminently reasonable pleas like requiring no-smoking sections on airplanes. Emboldened by that success, tobacco prohibitionists successfully campaigned for laws banning smoking on flights under two hours, then a ban on domestic flights altogether, then airports, restaurants, and buses. Now, they're working to have smoking banned at all but residences, and later, no doubt, they'll go after residences. Their agenda required a propaganda campaign to dupe the public with lies and distortions about some of the health effects of smoking. Had the tobacco prohibitionists made their full agenda known at the outset, they never would have succeeded in even getting no-smoking sections on airplanes.

This is precisely the strategy employed by the antigun lobby members. They start out with something eminently reasonable, such as a five-day waiting period before you can take delivery of a gun and restrictions against military automatic "assault" weapons. People who object to such a "reasonable" policy are made to be seen as unreasonable and reckless. But the waiting period is just the opening salvo against our Second Amendment rights. The next strategy is to call for licensing of gun owners. Then we'll see a ban on keeping a gun at home, requiring guns to be stored in a government armory. Then a ban on private ownership of guns. Like the tobacco prohibitionists, antigun advocates recruit what the communists called "useful idiots" to help them create and spread false and misleading propaganda about you.

"Williams," you say, "aren't you being a little unfair in assessing the good intentions of people like Sarah Brady?" Try this. See whether the antigun people would agree to amend the Brady bill with a sentence that goes like this: Neither Congress nor state legislatures shall enact any additional measures regulating the private ownership of guns. The antigun people would go ape and for a very good reason—it would threaten their ultimate plan to ban guns altogether.

The Second Amendment gives us the right to bear arms in order to have a "well-regulated militia." People with little understanding interpret that as meaning the National Guard or some other government organization. But here's how George Mason, one of our unsung framers, responded to the question, "I ask, sir, what is a militia?" saying, "It is the whole people, except for a few public officials." James Madison said, "Arms in the hands of citizens may be used at individual discretion . . . in private self-defense." George Washington said, "When firearms go, all else goes . . . we need them every hour." The framers of our Constitution knew well that an armed citizenry was the ultimate defense against government tyranny. As for crime, Thomas Paine said, "The peaceable part of mankind will be overrun by the vile and abandoned while they neglect the means of self-defense . . . [but] arms like laws discourage and keep the invader and plunderer in awe. . . . Horrid mischief would ensue were the good deprived of the use of them."

Our founders knew that government was the primary source of evil and oppression. Today's liberals wish to disarm us so they can run their evil and oppressive agenda on us. The fight against crime is just a convenient excuse to further their agenda. I don't know about you, but if you hear that Williams's guns have been taken, you'll know that Williams is dead.

Useful Idiots

April 6, 1994

Useful idiots was what wicked communists called decent, well-intentioned followers who bought their propaganda but had no understanding of their true agenda. That's what the typical American who calls himself an environmentalist is—a useful idiot for the movement's hardcore masters. "Whoa, Williams," you say, "environmentalists are America's caring people!"

How about some environmentalist quotations found in the late

Dixie Lee's book *Environmental Overkill*. Yale University professor LaMont Cole said, "To feed a starving child is to exacerbate the world overpopulation problem." Turner Broadcasting System's owner, Ted Turner, concurs, "Right now, there are just too many people on the planet. . . . When you look at us [Americans], we are a bunch of pigs . . . and losers."

How about honesty in the news? Barbara Pyle, CNN's environmental director, said, "I do have an ax to grind. . . . I want to be the little subversive person in television." The Boston *Globe*'s environmental reporter, Dianne Dumanski, says, "There is no such thing as objective reporting. . . . I've become even more crafty about finding the voices to say the things I think are true. That's my subversive mission." These and other reporters benefited from the teachings of Paul Watson, cofounder of Greenpeace: "It doesn't matter what's true; it only matters what people believe is true. . . . You are what the media define you to be. [Greenpeace] became a myth and a myth-generating machine."

Big media are dupes and coconspirators in helping us believe what's "true." During the Alar hoax, Ed Bradley of CBS's *60 Minutes*, commenting on Alar, told us, "The most potent cancer-causing agent in our food supply is a substance sprayed on apples to keep them on trees longer to make them look better." Phil Donahue chimed in, "Don't look now, but we're poisoning our kids." Guided by the Natural Resources Defense Council, most other members of the media panicked the public with the Alar lie.

America's socialists are just as inhumane as the former USSR's barbarians. We see this if we look back to their propaganda and public relations coup that culminated with a ban on DDT. Elizabeth Whelan's book *Toxic Terror: The Truth behind the Cancer Scares* cites numerous professional sources pointing out that DDT is a cheap and beneficial pesticide when used properly. Environmental gestapos, including the 1972 EPA director William Ruckelshaus, knew this, but that didn't stop them because there was an agenda.

Here's just one part of that agenda's results. In 1948, before DDT's widespread usage, Sri Lanka alone reported 2.8 million cases of malaria. With the usage of DDT, the number of malaria cases in 1963 dropped to 17. By 1969, following the ban on DDT, Sri Lanka's malaria cases rose again to 2.5 million. In terms of crop destruction and starvation, poor Third World countries have suffered mightily for

America's socialists—so much so that Thomas H. Jukes of the University of California at Berkeley was prompted to write, "The issue of banning DDT is unquestionably a genocidal one. . . . The balance is overwhelmingly in favor of DDT. . . . I refer you to the monumental bibliography of 3,404 references compiled by the Division of Biology and Agriculture."

The liberal agenda everywhere has a callous disregard for human rights. What's incomprehensible to me is the number of Americans ready to buy into Clinton's attempt to socialize medicine. If we fall for it, liberals will have the coup of this century. With the stroke of the presidential pen, one-seventh of our economy will be socialized. If you've been looking for a place to dig in your heels, this is it.

Attacking Private Property

APRIL 20, 1994

Henry Waxman, chairman of the House Energy and Commerce Subcommittee on Health, led an odious, contemptible, puritanical display of arrogance and power last week in hearings designed to intimidate tobacco company executives. The Waxman crowd and its tobacco prohibitionist allies are immune to common sense and have little respect for private property. How about our analyzing it?

For liberty-loving people, health effects from mainstream or secondhand tobacco smoke are not as important to the debate as property rights are. When there are private property rights, it's the owner who dominates the decision to use what in what way. You own your house; therefore, it's your decision whether smoking will be allowed. I own myself, and it's my decision to enter a house where smoking is allowed. Similarly, if I own a restaurant, business, or airline and permit smoking, it's your decision whether you'll be my customer or employee. My only obligation is that of informing you.

You protest, "Williams, that liberty business is OK, but what about the health costs smoking imposes on society?" Those costs are not a problem of liberty; they're a problem of socialism. If people get sick from smoking, or for that matter anything else, by what standard of morality should you be forced to pay for their treatment? There is none. But if we buy into the notion that because society bears the cost, we can dictate behavior, it won't be long before all liberty is lost. After all, my mom was right when she used to scold me when I was a child, saying, "As long as I'm paying the bills and I'm responsible for you, you're going to do what I say."

Homosexual and bisexual conduct is responsible for the AIDS epidemic, leading to the loss of thousands of lives and billions of dollars of costs to society. Should Congress ban homosexual behavior? Hundreds of thousands of Americans die or are disabled by heart attacks and coronary disease. Much of this costly health problem is caused by unhealthy diets and lifestyles. There's no nutritional need to add table salt to food. So, if you're in a restaurant and see a person putting salt on his food, why not take the saltshaker? Or, if you see a fat person spreading butter on his bread, why not take the butter and the bread? "Williams," you say, "Congress hasn't made a law about salt and butter! Plus, the salt and butter belong to the person." No matter. Should caring people wait for laws or be deterred by private property?

Even if tobacco companies did add more nicotine to cigarettes, as Waxman alleges, it would be precisely what smokers would want in the face of the tobacco prohibitionist movement. People generally prefer their vices in a diluted form: light beer, filtered cigarettes, and wine coolers. When do-gooders intervene with confiscatory taxes and bans, people switch to a more concentrated form of their vice. We cracked down on marijuana; now we have crack cocaine. When we prohibited alcohol, we got more white lightning. Producers prefer concentrated forms as well. It's much easier to conceal $50,000 worth of crack than $50,000 worth of marijuana.

Do-goodism has other pitfalls. When cigarettes are expensive, smokers not only want stronger cigarettes, so as to get the same bang for the buck, but smoke them down shorter. Both measures are less healthy, and the poorer you are, the more you'll do both. But this fact wouldn't deter Waxman and Clinton, and that's just my point. Statists are wicked people with an unbounded appetite for power and control. When they get finished with smokers, they'll be coming after you.

Financing Health Care Stupidly

JULY 20, 1994

Pretend automobile insurance is identical to traditional health care insurance. "There you go again, Williams," you say, "making false analogies. People are not cars!" That's right, but people aren't bricks either, and if a person and a brick came off the Empire State Building, both would obey the same laws of gravity. Similarly, auto and health expenditures both obey the same laws of supply and demand.

Your employer enrolls you in Blue Steel automobile insurance. When your car is "sick," you just take it into the shop and pay the $5 deductible and your mechanic sends the balance of the bill to Blue Steel. Under such a plan, what predictions would you make about changes in people's behavior?

What would the person do who had been getting a $150 tune-up once a year, a $30 oil change every 8,000 miles, and putting up with that deep fender scratch? If you predicted he'd get a tune-up and oil change more often and take his car to the finest body shop, go to the head of the class. But suppose you came across a person who insists, "I've been doing OK with a tune-up once a year and an oil change every 8,000 miles, and that scratch doesn't really bother me. When I have time, I'll buy some touch-up paint. There's no sense burdening our auto care system."

You'd probably offer a little lesson in economics, saying, "Look, if you don't use the car insurance, you still have the same money deducted from your pay. It pays you to use the mechanic as much as possible for any expenditure greater than $5. In other words, consider auto services greater than $5 free."

That's the demand side; people would overuse the system and not take the preventive care measures they'd otherwise employ. But what about the supply side? If auto insurance companies are to stay in business, they have several options. They may raise premiums, raise copayments, have a czar ration services by dictating what services are reimbursable, or some combination of these options. But if your employer is smart, he might underwrite an insurance plan like this: Two thousand dollars of the $4,000 of your earnings that went to purchase Blue Steel insurance could go to purchase insurance covering major losses like accidents or thefts. The other $2,000 could be put into an auto-dedicated tax-free savings account like an individual retirement account. You could withdraw that money, without tax penalty, for auto repairs and maintenance. Whatever you didn't spend could accumulate and be withdrawn tax-free at retirement.

This insurance plan produces a different class of incentives, among them greater preventive maintenance, more shopping around for good prices, and fewer demands for frivolous services. It eliminates most of the effects of "third-party" payer systems. That's some of what Senator Phil Gramm (R-Tex.) offered in his Comprehensive Family Health Access and Savings Act (SB 1807), originally developed by the Dallas-based National Center for Policy Analysis. Although marred by several defects, Senator Robert Dole's recent bill contains some of those elements.

Medical savings accounts are far superior to the Clinton crowd's agenda to socialize our medical care system, led by his health care point man, Senator Jay Rockefeller, who contemptuously said, "We're going to push through health care reform regardless of the views of the American people." Now how do you like those arrogant apples? I think they stink.

Science and Totalitarianism

November 2, 1994

Some of the world's most barbarous acts, from slavery to genocide, have been facilitated by bogus science. The Food and Drug Administration's Dr. David Kessler along with Representative Henry Waxman and Environmental Protection Agency head Carol Browner are modern-day leaders of that ugly scheme. Don't get me wrong; I'm not equating them to Hitler. But what distinguishes them is a matter of degree but not kind. In pursuit of their vision of what's a "desirable" society, they seek to abrogate private property rights, personal liberty, and rule of law, using bogus science to justify their actions. Just as decent Germans built a Trojan horse for Hitler to take over, decent Americans are doing the same for a future tyrant. Let's look at some of the bogus science used by Dr. Kessler and his accomplices in their pursuit of a "desirable" society—one that is smoke-free.

Kessler's attempt to equate nicotine in cigarettes with other addictive drugs is fraud. Traditional definitions of addiction include intoxication. The behavioral effects of tobacco differ fundamentally from addicting drugs like cocaine, heroin, and alcohol. Ask yourself, "Which pilot would you like to fly you—one who's had a couple of cigarettes, a couple of snorts of cocaine or heroin, or a couple of martinis?" Give me the cigarette smoker. Cigarette smoking is more properly labeled a habit, like coffee consumption. Habits may be difficult to break. Cigarette smokers who attempt to break the habit often suffer the same fate of many fat people who work hard and lose weight only to gain it back again and then try again.

Dr. Kessler's able accomplice is EPA head Carol Browner. When Browner classified environmental tobacco smoke (ETS) as a group-A carcinogen, just like benzene and asbestos, her actions were based on grossly fraudulent and dishonest statistical methodology. Twenty-four of the thirty studies the EPA reviewed reported no statistically significant ETS–lung cancer relationship. Of the eleven studies done by U.S. scientists, not one reported significant cancer risk. The EPA was aware of and ignored similar findings of the two largest and most recent studies on ETS–lung cancer (Stockwell 1992; Brownson 1992, sponsored by the National Cancer Institute).

But the EPA may not get away with its lies. The U.S. District Court for North Carolina recently ruled in *Flue-Cured Tobacco Cooperative v. EPA* that the plaintiffs could proceed with a court challenge to the EPA's designation of "secondhand" cigarette smoke as a known carcinogen. Plaintiffs argued that the EPA lacks statutory authority to issue that designation. Moreover, it's based on EPA data manipulation it knows to be false. The EPA didn't challenge Flue-Cured's allegation of data manipulation. Instead, it tried to get the court to dismiss the suit on the grounds that federal law does not permit judicial review of federal designation of a product as carcinogenic. The court disagreed, saying it does have that right and that, because the EPA's declaration has led to banning of cigarette smoking in thousands of public and private establishments, it is "ripe" for review.

That's why Hitler in Germany, the parliament in apartheid South Africa, and tyrants elsewhere hate judicial review of legislative or quasi-legislative acts. And so do Browner, Kessler, and Waxman.

Whether you hate smokers or not, Americans must reject bogus science and attacks on the principle of rule of law, personal liberty, and private property as a means to achieve a "desirable" society. If we permit it against smokers, you can rest assured that somebody else with another vision will use the same Trojan horse in pursuit of his objectives.

THE
INTERNATIONAL
SCENE

The most significant recent development on the international scene has been the collapse of the Soviet Union. If there's any one individual who we can thank for this momentous event, it's President Ronald Reagan. It was he who, in the face of opposition at home and abroad, decided to give the "evil empire" the back-breaking challenge of seeing what a real arms race was about. It was Ronald Reagan who initiated the Strategic Defense Initiative, dubbed "Star Wars" by the hostile media and our left-leaning academia. Ultimately, the Soviet Union had much greater faith in our technological superiority than we ourselves had. Much of the collapse of the Soviet Union stems from the fact that its moribund economy would not allow it to compete in a real arms race and feed its people at the same time. Plus, it was altogether hopeless to keep up with us technologically. Contrary to the vision of the "peaceniks," the end of the cold war was achieved through military strength rather than through appeasement, peace negotiations, and phony arms agreements.

Along with the collapse of the Soviet Union, the world has been discovering the horrors of communism that for eight decades had been covered up and apologized for by the elite in this country and abroad. We are only now beginning to get the full story of the unspeakable horrors in Romania, Yugoslavia, and East Germany. We are only now *learning how the Russians suppressed and divided the Soviet Union's many ethnic groups. In fact, Verwoed and the other architects of South Africa's apartheid system, which never was successful, were, I'm sure, green with envy over the Soviets' system of ethnic division and suppression that was managed under the name of the "policy of the nationalities."*

The other big international issue of the decade was South Africa. South Africa's system of systematic denial of basic human rights to its colored and Asian population was an abomination and rightfully made it the world's pariah nation. With Nelson Mandela as president there are greater human rights protections and a semblance of democracy.

South Africa's horrible apartheid system has now been dismantled. The task today for South Africans is finding something to replace apartheid. This question cannot be taken lightly because the overriding tendency in human history is for one evil to be replaced by another far worse. After all, the injustices of the czars were replaced by those of Stalin, which were much worse. The injustices of Chiang Kai-shek were replaced with those of Mao Tse-tung. The injustices of Batista in Cuba were replaced by those of Castro. Those of Somoza were replaced by those of the Sandinistas. Injustices of the shah of Iran were replaced by those of the ayatollah. And all over Africa, the injustices of the colonial powers were replaced by the unspeakable cruelties of black tyrants. It should not be assumed that injustice will be automatically replaced by justice. The supreme tragedy would be if, two or three decades from now, the ordinary black South African could say that he was better off under apartheid. Clearly, many of his neighbors to the north can say they were more secure and had a higher standard of living.

The columns in this section discuss topics ranging from communism and South Africa to Third World poverty and international trade.

The Evil Empire

JANUARY 17, 1990

Intellectuals and other elite have been pulling a giant snow job on Americans since the end of World War II. Communism, we were told, was the wave of the future; it was more humane than capitalism; it was a workers' paradise. When President Ronald Reagan denounced the Soviet Union and its empire as the focal point of world evil, he aroused a storm of elite protest and was accused of warmongering.

The maliciousness of communism can no longer be concealed. People who've lived under communism are putting their lives on the line, openly giving it a thumbs-down. We wonder how long the brutal regimes of Red China, North Korea, and Cuba can hold out. We wonder how long Africans, particularly those struggling against South Africa's apartheid, will view communism as their savior. We also wonder how much longer Marxist college professors in the United States will attempt to indoctrinate our youth with the "wonders" of communism before the students walk out en masse.

It took World War II for the world to recognize that Naziism is inherently evil. Recent events have demonstrated that communism is also inherently evil. But the big lesson is for naught if we see the evils of Naziism and communism as residing only in despicable characters like Hitler, Stalin, Castro, Ceausescu, Mao Tse-tung, and their henchmen. While it's true that in most political systems the scum rises to the top, the larger question is, How does such a brutal system evolve in the first place?

The throne on which most tyrants sit is custom-built by decent people—people who, like many of us in America, pine for "social justice." For them, justice is not measured by a neutral rule-of-law process, whereby the law treats all equally and government officials are not above the law. For them, justice is determined by a particular set of societal results; their language consists of terms like *social responsibility, social goals,* and *targets.*

High on their agenda is income. People differ; some have mental, physical, or entrepreneurial talents whereby they earn more than others. Politically generated envy causes some to fall easy prey to demagogues who convince them they have less income because someone else has more. Politicians are given carte blanc to confiscate income in the name of promoting social justice. The leading items on the political agenda are attacks on private property and calls for expanded government power. That's why the principles of private property and limited government are an abomination to tyrants everywhere, whether in the Soviet Union, Red China, or the U.S. Congress.

Once socialist goals are established—whether it's income equality, agriculture or steel output targets, or socialized medicine—private property rights and individual liberty are seen as impediments. If they stand in the way of the socialist agenda, they must be brutally suppressed. Decent people lack the ruthlessness required to attain their goals; therefore, the scum that has risen to the top takes over and does the dirty work, often going to unforeseen lengths.

Communism is inherently evil because individual liberty and property rights are suppressed while government power is unlimited. Individual liberty stands in permanent irreconcilable conflict with its goals. This was seen by Alexis de Tocqueville, who said, "Socialism seeks equality in restraint and servitude."

The learned editors at *Time* magazine designated Gorbachev as Man of the Decade when all he's done is not stamp the iron boot (so far) on the people's thirst for liberty. They might have designated Adolf Hitler in his time had the German people rebelled against Nazi oppression.

Destroyed Lecture Notes

FEBRUARY 27, 1990

It's unprofessional to solicit pity, but here's a cast just begging for sympathy. The worst disaster for a professor is to have his lecture notes destroyed. In my case, twenty-two years of teaching have produced rich lecture notes with plenty of anecdotes, data, examples, and tricky questions, which, if lost, would be hard to replace.

My lecture notes are safe, so it's not a case of personal pity. The pity is earned by Marxist professors who've been roguishly brainwashing and lying to our youth for decades. Their lecture notes have been so decimated by recent events in Eastern Europe that they might easily qualify for disaster relief.

Their notes contain pages of tirades against U.S. imperialism and oppression. But the cat is out of the bag; the world now knows that Russia is ringed by captive nations, such as Lithuania, Estonia, Latvia, and Armenia, who are now threatening unilateral declarations of independence. Our Marxist professors must discard their notes and substitute: Russia is the world's cruelest and last colonial power. They may seek to explain, evade, or deny the cruelty of Marxism-Leninism and make claims of its success in Cuba, China, and North Korea, but there's no getting around the facts or the corpses.

Marxist professors led campus struggles for disinvestment and sanctions against South Africa, portraying communism as a friend to the black struggle against apartheid. They make no mention of how previous Russian rulers Vladimir Lenin and Joseph Stalin created an ethnic homeland policy that South Africa's Hendrik Verwoerd would have envied. The Russian program is called the "policy of the nationalities." Different ethnic groups are required to live in certain places, and laws are passed restricting travel.

Marxist professors lecture our youth that communism is "the wave of the future" and that in the "workers' paradise" there is no want because "from each according to his ability and to each according to his needs." Of course, no mention is made of the scarcity of soap, toilet paper, and adequate heat. In Marxism 101, professors preach the Marxist cry "Working men of all countries, unite," for you "have nothing to lose but your chains." Try telling that to Romanians and Lithuanians.

How about the Marxist claim of no privileged classes, unlike those that exist in the evil United States. If the profs try that this semester, the students should list all of Romanian president Nicolae Ceausescu's finery and the pampered lifestyles of the other communist bosses.

These are just a few of the lies that flourish full-blown in some of our most prestigious schools, such as Harvard, Yale, Stanford, Dartmouth, and Brown, where parents have coughed up $20,000 or more to see their youngsters indoctrinated with unadulterated flimflam. Worse yet, we have members of Congress spewing similar blather about the moral equivalency of capitalism and communism.

We have our news media burning a path to communist countries to give us testimonials of deprivation and atrocities. You'd think they'd also fish up a few of our campus and congressional communists and query, "You've been preaching about the wonders of communism; could you reconcile your outlook with those who've actually lived under communism?"

Our sympathies go to the Marxist professors who've had their lecture notes destroyed and who must now tell students Ronald Reagan was right: Communism is headed for the dustbin of history. Socialism is headed in the same direction. After all, socialism is the same as communism but with a happy face.

We'd feel even greater pity for our Marxist professors if a Romanian happened to become president of Harvard, Stanford, or Yale. If this happened at the University of Massachusetts, there's a real chance of Marxist professors being Ceausescued.

War and Peace

APRIL 10, 1991

The most mindless bumper sticker is the one that intones "If you want peace, work for justice." Let's think about war and peace.

The normal state of the world is war somewhere. Don't just take my word; pick a century. Do treaties prevent war? In this century alone, there were at least ten major peace treaties, but they didn't stop the destruction of tens of millions of lives. Treaties and disarmament pacts simply gave aggressors the time to build armies and the nerve to attack. Who's ready to say that war is the result of poorly worded peace treaties and disarmament agreements? Who is willing to bet it's going to be this generation that succeeds in treaty writing where others have failed?

There's considerable evidence to support the proposition that military might and preparedness is a much greater war deterrent than treaties and disarmament agreements. Europe is now going through its longest period of continuous peace. Do we want to chalk it up to treaties? Or do we want to chalk it up to the fact that, since World War II,

Europe has been an armed camp bristling with weapons of mass destruction? Armed aggression would have meant intolerable losses.

People who attribute the cold war's end to a change of heart in the Kremlin might want to think that one over again. Instead, we can thank Reagan's military buildup for the changes in Eastern Europe. Russia found that it simply could not compete effectively in an arms race against us. Moreover, even trying to compete came at a huge cost to the standard of living of its people. The straw that broke the Russian bear's back was the Strategic Defense Initiative, ridiculed by America's leftists as "Star Wars." The liberal media and the Union of Concerned Scientists said that we couldn't develop a defense against missile attack. But the Kremlin had greater confidence in our ability to build an effective missile defense. Maybe their spies were peeking at Patriots.

Here's where we are now. America already has the means and capacity to deploy modified versions of the Patriot missile and space interceptors known as "brilliant pebbles." If Jerusalem can be protected against enemy missiles, why not New York, Chicago, and Los Angeles? Our ability to protect ourselves is not one of means but of will. The U.S. Congress is far more interested in using tax dollars to buy votes, through a variety of handout programs, than it is in performing its constitutional function of providing for the national defense. It seems as though it would much rather expose us to a terrorist missile attack than to cut the $30 billion plus handout to farmers.

We, the people, had better change this soon. According to Central Intelligence Agency estimates, in ten years or so there will be twenty nations capable of delivering crude nuclear weapons. You can rest assured that if Saddam Hussein had the means, he'd threaten to use a nuclear weapon on us. Yes, we'd turn any country that attacked us into a trash heap, but that wouldn't bring back tens of thousands of American lives lost.

Now that the Middle East war is over, the first order of business for the White House is to go on the offensive to get Congress to appropriate funds for development and deployment of President Reagan's Strategic Defense Initiative. You say, "Williams, the ABM treaty prohibits that!" I say, What good are treaties if they aren't broken when it's expedient to do so?

Nineteen Ninety-one Nonsense

DECEMBER 25, 1991

We improve the future by serious attention to mistakes of the past. Let's look at 1991 nonsense. The 1991 prize for treasonous stupidity goes to all those congressmen who decried Bush's Desert Storm military buildup, saying sanctions should be given a chance. We now know that Iraq was much closer to developing a nuclear weapon than anybody had anticipated. Had we listened to those congressmen and their lament to give sanctions a chance, Saddam Hussein might have had nuclear weapons to use against our troops. Might these be the same congressmen who previously tried to scuttle funding for Patriot missiles?

Because of the incredibly malicious and stupid 1990 budget deal, 1991 ends as a recession year. Remember the talk and the glee on the faces of the president and his men and congressmen after having legislated the largest peacetime tax increase in our history? We were told that their budget deal would eliminate the five-year $500 billion deficit. I told you then they were lying. The deficit was not reduced. Spending was increased. Now the five-year deficit is over $1 trillion.

In one fell swoop, Congress destroyed economic growth and eliminated thousands of jobs. Congress gets away with stupid policy because we're suckers for the politics of envy. Whenever Congress promises to soak the rich, like fools, we believe it. As a result, the few rich go about their business, and the 99 percent of the rest of us are screwed. Remember how Senator George Mitchell pushed through a 10 percent luxury tax on expensive cars, boats, and airplanes. He thought the rich were immune to the laws of demand and would buy the same number of these luxury items. It didn't turn out that way. The National Marine Manufacturers Association reports that boat sales are down 60 percent and that nineteen thousand boat workers lost their jobs. Luxury auto sales are down 20 percent, and three thousand salesmen have lost their jobs. The luxury tax destroyed jobs and reduced revenue to the Treasury.

In my more cynical moments, I think that we Americans deserve what Congress does to us; we ask for it. Despite congressmen's ineptitude and lies in handling the budget, despite their previous Gramm-Rudman lies promising a balanced budget in 1991, despite their writing bad checks and walking away from the congressional restaurant without paying their bills, despite their clandestine salary increases, you and I are increasingly willing to allow them to control precious areas of our lives like education and child care. Now Americans beg Congress to take over our health care. That's incredibly ignorant and shortsighted. What makes us think that congressmen can do a better job managing our health than they've done with the budget, national debt, and education, not to mention management of their own lives? If we fall for national health care, and years from now, when health care has many more problems, I'm going to say I told you so and we deserve it.

What should our agenda be for 1992? Here are the guidelines. First, we need a new president, one with integrity and guts to at least stick by his promises. Without my endorsing anyone, we might look at Pete Dupont, former governor of Delaware. Second, Americans need to get surly about rising regulation and taxes at the federal, state, and local levels of government. Third, Americans need to find a good way to tell whether a politician is lying. The way I see it, the best overall indication is to look to see whether his lips are moving. If they are, he's lying.

Trade Deficit Nonsense

JANUARY 29, 1992

Our balance of trade with Japan is balanced. That's the good news. The bad news is that our intellectual midgets—congressmen—cannot understand that. The best single brief analysis of the issue can be found in an article by John D. Fargo, writing in the October 1991 issue of *Freeman*, a publication of the Foundation for Economic Education headquartered in Irvington, New York.

A trade balance sheet has two accounts: the current account, consisting of goods and services exchanged, and the capital account, consisting of stocks, bonds, and investments. As such, the trade balance sheet must always be balanced. Let's look at it.

Scenario 1: Japan sells us $100 million worth of Hondas. If it bought $100 million worth of rice from us, we'd all agree there would be no trade deficit; the current trade account would be balanced.

Scenario 2: Suppose Japan sold us $100 million worth of Hondas and, instead of buying rice, used the $100 million to build a factory in Kentucky. We'd have a $100 million deficit on current account offset by a $100 million surplus (buying something) on the capital account—a balance. Instead of creating American jobs by buying rice, jobs would be created by the factory in Kentucky.

Scenario 3: The Japanese sell us $100 million worth of Hondas but neither buy rice nor build a factory in Kentucky but instead deposit $100 million in a U.S. bank. Again, we have a $100 million deficit on current account and a $100 million surplus (buying something, in this case a bank account) on the capital account. Instead of creating jobs by buying rice or building a factory, the Japanese create jobs by making money available for loans for Americans to buy homes or American firms to build new plants or invest in new equipment.

Scenario 4: The Japanese sell us $100 million worth of Hondas (current account deficit). They neither buy rice nor build a factory nor deposit it in a U.S. bank but buy something already existing, such as the Rockefeller Center or MGM Studios (capital account surplus). The American who got the $100 million may use it to build a new factory in Kentucky or lend it to people to invest, thereby creating jobs.

Next-to-the-last scenario: Honda sells us $100 million worth of cars (current account deficit) but takes the dollars back to Japan. Dollars cannot be spent in Japan, so what might happen? A British firm may sell the Japanese wool. Instead of being paid in yen, they'd be paid with the $100 million proceeds from the Honda sale. The British firm might use those dollars to purchase U.S. Treasury notes (capital account surplus).

Last scenario: This is the one politicians believe and the one I'd actually like, if true. Honda sells us $100 million worth of cars. It buys nothing, and just for the love of dollars, the Japanese keep them stashed in a national cookie jar. Japanese manufacturers work their fannies off just so Americans can be supplied with all sorts of goodies in exchange for slips of paper manufactured by the U.S. mint. That would be wonderful. We Americans could relax and bask in the sun while the Japanese slave to supply cars, cameras, and all sorts of high-tech goods in exchange for slips of paper sporting pictures of famous U.S. presidents. Sorry, I'm afraid the Japanese are not that stupid.

"OK, Williams," you say, "but I don't like the Japanese buying up America!" The fact is that Britain and the Netherlands have much more invested in our country. What's more, if the Japanese get mad at us, are they going to pick up the Rockefeller Center and take it home with them?

Government-Created Poverty

APRIL 19, 1994

I've visited a number of poor countries. In countries like South Africa, Mexico, Brazil, Jamaica, and the Bahamas, poor people are unimaginably poorer than our poor people. But you don't have to be in those countries long before you develop an appreciation for their rich entrepreneurial spirit. In some cases, you see that sprit when you get through customs and are bombarded by people selling everything from food, watches, and clothing to taxi rides and tours. With that spirit, you really have to wonder why they're still poor.

A large part of the responsibility for the grinding Third World poverty lies with their governments. Jamaica has a serious transportation problem. Entrepreneurial Jamaicans could buy minivans to provide jitney services. But because of the government's policy of granting restrictive and exclusive import licenses, plus taxes, a minivan that could be purchased here for $16,000 might cost a Jamaican close to $50,000. Similar handicaps can be found in many other areas of potential business ownership.

Take South Africa. Here is a country faced with great political pressures for economic development. You'd think it would welcome its citizens importing U.S. computer software programs, mobile and portable telephones, educational equipment, and other high-tech goods. However, in many cases, there are high tariffs and, in some cases, outright prohibition on their importation—talk about shooting yourself in the foot.

In many countries, most notably those in South America and Africa, in order for a person to get into the simplest business, such as being a seamstress, requires hurdling a system of impossible regulations and official corruption where bribes and kickbacks are the order of the day. Plus, the simple tools required for the business are likely to cost multiples of what an American businessman pays.

When you see the robust entrepreneurial spirit in some of these countries, you can easily understand why these people are such successes when they immigrate to the United States. Because these countries are too poor to have our kind of welfare, the people must work to survive. That necessity, coupled with a greater measure of economic freedom, helps explain their success in our country. Therefore, we observe the seemingly perplexing phenomena: Indians tend to do well everywhere except India; Vietnamese do well everywhere except Vietnam. As for Jamaicans and other Caribbean people, when they come to the United States, they manage to earn a family income higher than that of the average American.

For the world's poor to become more prosperous, they need a greater measure of economic liberty. You can prove this several ways. Most American immigrants hit these shores poor. We were a Third World country. There was no foreign aid. What we had going for us was a large measure of economic liberty. There weren't the economic roadblocks found in many countries today. A simpler proof of the benefits of economic liberty comes if you list today's most prosperous countries. Rich countries like the United States, Hong Kong, and Japan have a large measure of economic liberty, whereas countries with grinding poverty, such as Brazil, Mexico, and most of Africa, have extensive government control and regulation of the economy.

During my visits, I found that the elite and politicians feed their poor people the same attention-diverting line fed by our elite. They say more handouts (foreign aid) are needed. They blame the poverty on colonialism. That's just like our elite, who address poverty by calling for handouts and blaming racism. The last thing both elite propose is economic liberty and the right to be free from government interference.

Let's Not Declare Justice Yet

MAY 4, 1994

The sight of South Africa's black citizens in voting lines for the first time in their history is a joy to behold. Apartheid, which was never as successful as its designer, Hendrick Verwoed, envisioned, is now gone, and blacks have a say in the politics of their country. But our joy should be tempered. After all, didn't we witness the same jubilation when Zaire, Rwanda, and Burundi won their independence from Belgium in the early 1960s and when the British colonies of Tanzania and Uganda won their independence in 1961 and 1962? Postindependence history for these and most other African nations hasn't been pleasant.

Today's slaughter in Rwanda and Burundi is simply the latest episode of a periodic affair. In 1972, an estimated 200,000 Hutus were slaughtered by the Tutsis. In 1988, 35,000, mostly Hutus, were killed in the period of a month. Many victims didn't die painlessly, by way of bullets and bombs. They met their deaths through dismemberment, hacking, and decapitation.

Then there's Milton Obote and Idi Amin Dada in Uganda, whose reign of terror resulted in as many as 1 million deaths due to "ethnic cleansing." In varying degrees, gross human rights violations are Africa's daily fare, including black slavery in the Sudan and Mauritania.

But brutal regimes are only part of the tragedy of postindependence Africa. In 1987, according to the Washington-based Population Crisis Committee, of the eleven countries with the worst human suffering, ten were African. Before independence, virtually every colony was agriculturally self-sufficient. Since independence, as a result of government policy, food production has been declining at rates as high as 15 percent a year. Of the forty-one black African nations, only Botswana and Senegal permit freedom of expression and criticism of government policies. Three nations, Senegal, Botswana, and Mauritius, grant their people the right to vote and choose their leaders.

Most African countries are kleptocracies in which politicians enrich themselves at the expense of their people. President Mobutu Sese Seko of Zaire, the world's poorest country, has a conservatively estimated wealth of between $8 billion and $11 billion. Emperor Bokassa, the former president of the Central African Republic, was reputed to own twelve mansions in France.

South Africa, like its neighbors to the north, has the full potential for ethnic strife. There are long-standing animosities between the eight million Zulus, Mangosuthu Buthelezi's people, and Nelson Mandela's Xhosa peoples, which number nearly four million. There are about four million northern and southern Sothos and nearly two million Tswanas and other black ethnic groups. Adding to that volatile mixture are roughly three million coloreds, plus one million Indians, who are hated and mistreated all over Africa. Then there's the long-standing, though quiet, antagonism and distrust between Afrikaners and British.

Given the history of the continent, it isn't sufficient for South Africans to eliminate apartheid—they must decide on its replacement. The normal course of history is that one injustice tends to be replaced by one far worse. Injustices of the czars were replaced by those of Stalin; injustices of Chiang Kai-shek were replaced with Mao's; those of the shah of Iran with Khomeini's, Batista's with Castro's, and Somoza's with the Sandinistas'. All over Africa, colonial injustices were replaced by those of dictators.

Despite the historical odds, there's a note of optimism. South Africans have been negotiating their freedom while communism has collapsed; they're aware of their northern neighbors' experiences. And, surprisingly, there's considerable racial goodwill between blacks and whites.

Liberal Visions of Injustice

AUGUST 3, 1994

Conservative estimates put the Rwandan genocidal slaughter at 300,000. Disease and famine threaten another million. We're all horrified by the scenes on television. But there's little that's new about it. It's just that we've been distracted by a more unacceptable form of injustice—the mistreatment of blacks by whites in South Africa.

Watusis are a tall Nilotic people who came down from the north and subjugated the Hutu people. In 1959, Hutus (90 percent of the population in Rwanda) overthrew their feudal masters, killing some 100,000 Watusis. In 1972, in neighboring Burundi, Hutus rebelled against Watusi oppression. Mindful of the genocide in Rwanda, the Watusis set out to slaughter those Hutus who were government workers or had money or education. Hutu children were taken out of schools and had their heads smashed with sledgehammers. When it was all over, nearly 200,000 Hutus were dead. In 1988, Watusis went on another rampage, ending with 20,000 Hutus dead. Some estimates put the death toll at 38,000. In all these conflicts, death didn't always come quickly. People were dismembered, decapitated, hacked to death, or burned.

While this was going on, what was the focal point of liberals' outrage? You guessed it. They were on their moral high horse protesting white injustices in South Africa. By any standard, South African injustices were trivial compared to those in other African countries. Between 1910 and 1975, no more than 10,000 South African blacks lost their lives in civil conflict with government. Plus, nobody died from hacking, dismemberment, burning, or decapitation. Liberal lack of outrage against black barbarism displays an attitude differing little from one that says that blacks brutalizing other blacks is acceptable but that whites mistreating blacks is intolerable because whites are held accountable to civilized standards of behavior. That's the liberals' domestic attitude as well.

But it's not just Rwanda/Burundi's gross human rights abuses that were ignored by liberals. Uganda's Idi Amin, Milton Obote, and Tito Okello conducted a reign of terror that ended nearly a million lives. By the time Equatorial Guinea's Macias Nguema was overthrown in 1979, he had massacred one-seventh of that tiny nation's population. According to Professor George Ayittey at American University, at least 6 million Africans have perished since 1960. More than 5.4 million have been made refugees, which doesn't include 13 million internally displaced persons. Barbarism and human rights abuses have been so unthinkable that South Africa, despite its apartheid, became home to thousands of refugees.

"Minor" African abuses include deportation of Indians and Arabs in Kenya, Tanzania, Zambia, Zanzibar, and Malawi. Mauritania outlawed slavery in 1980; however, many blacks are still slaves. Thousands of Dinkas have been taken into slavery by Sudan's Muslim population. Here's one for harebrained college professors who teach moral equivalency between Western values and others: In the Sudan, under Islamic law (*sharia*), theft is punishable by chopping off the left hand. If a weapon is used, it's the left hand and right foot. Between 1983 and 1985, several hundred men were punished that way; blasphemy is punishable by crucifixion. In the Sudan, Mali, Chad, and several other countries to a lesser degree, millions of girls suffer the horror of genital mutilation.

Western governments are a major contributor to Africa's tragedy. Corrupt governments might have fallen, but with foreign aid, they've been able to buy friends, silence critics, and purchase arms to use against their own people. Only Africans can solve their immense problems. The best long-term help the West can give is to eliminate trade barriers, mind its business, and keep its money.

THE LAW
& SOCIETY

Along with the decline of rule of law and respect for private property, there has been a remarkable and steady growth in criminal activity. Our society has demonstrated little desire to protect itself from criminals who prey on its law-abiding community. Indeed, it often appears as though it is the criminal who has the protections of the law and the sympathy of the criminal justice system, rather than the law-abiding citizen.

Bureau of Justice statistics show that the median murder sentence is fifteen years but that the median release time is five years. The typical sentence for rape is eight years, but rapists are out in three. For robbery and assault, typical sentences are six and four years, but the villains are out in two and one, respectively. Fifty-one percent of violent criminals are out in two years or less, and 76 percent are out in three. More than 60 percent of these released violent offenders are re-arrested within three years for a serious crime. Judges hand down tough sentences just to mollify and deceive the public; behind closed doors criminals are secretly turned loose on us. Our society will continue to suffer the high cost of crime until we decide to protect ourselves from malicious predators. Some of the columns that follow address our growing crime problem and what might be done about it.

Other columns in this section focus on how we have replaced methods and practices that worked with those that sound good. We have replaced individual accountability with "social" accountability. We al-

*lowed people deemed misfits and parasites yesteryear, and treated ac-
cordingly, to become society's mascots. In the process, we have turned
ourselves into a nation of victims and have given up many liberties to
government in the name of protection.*

Coddling Criminals

OCTOBER 24, 1990

Why do people own more pocket calculators? Why do people use less
oil? We don't have to consult an expert to give us a dose of psychobabble. It's simple and obvious: The cost of pocket calculators has fallen,
and the cost of oil has risen. People are behaving just as the law of
demand predicts.

Here's another simple question: Why has crime, hoodlumism, and
wanton property destruction risen? Depending on the "expert," you'll
get such psychosociobabble as poverty, discrimination, Vietnam,
Reagan, the time, and assorted other nonsense. But the true cause is
simple: The cost of crime, hoodlumism, and wanton property destruction has fallen. Let's look at it.

In some cities, a teenage hoodlum can be arrested up to seventeen
times on misdemeanor, even felony, charges before he spends one night
in jail. He's "counseled and released" to the custody of his parents. He
laughs at the law, but, more devastatingly, he becomes living evidence
to his peers that laws can be ignored at very little cost. Years ago, a
judge might have declared such a hoodlum incorrigible and sentenced
him to a term in reform school until he became an adult. Today, through
the miracle of psychosociobabble, judges see the habitual hoodlum as a
victim to be spared from the dictates of a civilized society.

It's the same story with adult criminals. They commit armed robbery, rape, and murder. District attorneys (DAs) plea bargain the offense down to simple robbery, assault, and voluntary or involuntary
manslaughter. Often this is done with neither the knowledge nor the
consent of the victim. A quirk that allows DAs to get away with such
atrocities is the fact that, in criminal matters, the state is the plaintiff

and the victim has little say in the prosecution of the case. More often than not, criminals receive short sentences and, if they receive longer sentences—like life in prison—they're out on the streets in seven years or less. In states like California, nearly 50 percent of inmates entering prison were on probation or parole at the time of their crime. Older people recall the term *three-time loser*, which is gone from today's vocabulary, wherein judges would sentence habitual criminals to life in prison.

The criminal huggers might ask, "Williams, our jails are overcrowded; where are we going to put the criminals?" Fly across our country, and you'll see plenty of space. Besides, the United States has territorial possessions in the Pacific that can be made to alleviate our jail overcrowding. We lack the will, not the space.

Some huggers might argue that it's too costly to build jails, pointing out that each inmate costs $25,000 a year. I say it's more costly not to build jails. The average criminal costs us at least $100,000 a year in losses from burglaries, arson, robbery, and grand theft, auto. And that doesn't include intangible costs, such as personal trauma from rape, assault, and the loss of loved ones. Neither does it include the cost of protection, including security services, locks, bars, and the inconveniences we suffer such as fear and having to have exact change. Considering these costs, the $25,000 to keep a criminal behind bars is quite a bargain.

Protecting us from criminals is the major function of local, state, and federal government. And they have failed miserably in that role. The primary reason for that failure is that politicians have given a higher priority to things they shouldn't be doing. Short of politicians making crime more costly, citizens will have to raise the cost by arming themselves. "Williams," you say, "that's a Dodge City mentality." I say check Dodge City's record; when everybody owned a gun there was less crime. We must instill fear in those who would prey on others.

Double Jeopardy

MARCH 17, 1993

The Los Angeles–based Reason Foundation's flagship publication, *Reason* magazine, has an interesting commentary in its April edition titled "Try, Try Again," by Jacob Sullum. It's about the federal trial of the four police officers acquitted by a Simi Valley jury of using excessive force in the arrest of Rodney King. When the 333 prospective jurors showed up at the federal courthouse, they were given a fifty-three-page questionnaire that included such questions as "What was your reaction to the verdicts in the state court trial?" "What do you feel caused the civil unrest and riots that occurred in Los Angeles in April and May of 1992?" "Do you fear the prospect of social unrest following a verdict in this case?"

Sullum says, and convincingly so, that such questions make it clear that the retrial is not about justice but about getting it "right" this time. The politically correct first order of business is that the jurors' decision must not cause another riot in Los Angeles. Second, the trial "must restore faith" in the criminal justice system. It's only a trivial matter whether the trial violates our Constitution's Fifth Amendment prohibition that says, "Nor shall any person be subject for the same offense to be twice put in jeopardy of his life or limb."

Slick gestapo federal prosecutors will tell us that the second trial doesn't constitute double jeopardy because, in the first trial, the police were charged with assault. The charge this time is violation of Rodney King's right to be free from unreasonable force, to be safe while in custody, and not to be punished without a trial. This charge is simply legal sleight of hand. The first trial jury found the police officers not guilty of assault or excessive force. The federal jury has to reject the finding of the Simi Valley verdict in order to find the L.A. cops guilty of violating King's civil rights. In other words, the federal court is actually trying the officers on the same charges. They will use facts presented in the first trial to determine whether the officers assaulted and used excessive force on Rodney King.

Congress intended the law under which the officers were charged to be a guard against corrupt law enforcement (especially in the Old South). If local authorities rigged a trial, the feds can and should come in. That makes sense because if there were corruption it would be as if no trial took place. But no one has argued that corrupt officials rigged the Simi Valley trial or that there was jury tampering. The closest thing to jury tampering was the pretrial contact made by the NAACP that led to the disqualification of four black jurors in the Simi Valley jury pool, a fact that was also concealed by the media.

Sarcastically, Sullum says that the earlier trial was rigged in the sense that "the defendants were presumed innocent, and the prosecutor had to prove its case beyond a reasonable doubt." This federal trial, which is little more than a kangaroo court, has presumed the defendants guilty; all that remains is to find a way to politely trump up something.

For those who saw only the video of the Rodney King beating, the police appear to be guilty; they were surprised by the verdict. But that's just like those of us who watched former D.C. mayor Marion Barry smoke crack and were surprised by the verdict. Do we want mob rule or what amounts to the same thing—the federal kangaroo court now in process in Los Angeles? Or should we accept the imperfections of the jury system? If it's the former, why don't we be more honest and simply lynch those L.A. cops?

Criminal Leaks

FEBRUARY 2, 1994

The Washington-based Heritage Foundation commissioned James Wootton, president of Safe Streets Alliance, to write a report on "Truth in Sentencing." Here are some of its findings.

Remember twelve-year-old Polly Klaas's kidnapping and murder, which angered us all? Her alleged assailant was paroled last June after serving eight years of a sixteen-year sentence for kidnapping.

Former Chicago Bull Michael Jordan had to bury his murdered father last July. Charged in his murder are Larry Demery and Daniel

Green. Demery had been charged in three previous cases involving theft. Green was on parole after having served only two years of a six-year sentence for assaulting a man with an ax.

Sister Mary Glinka was strangled to death at her convent. In 1979, Melvin Jones, her alleged assailant, had been sentenced in North Carolina to eighteen to twenty years for voluntary manslaughter. He escaped in 1986, was arrested in Baltimore for three burglaries, and was paroled in 1990. In 1991, North Carolina sentenced him to a year for prison escape and later that year contacted Maryland officials to arrange for him to be paroled in Maryland.

These three cases demonstrate our criminal justice system's callous disregard for law-abiding citizens. The members of the parole boards that freed these men are directly responsible for the deaths of these three people and the pain and suffering of the victims' families and friends. Had these criminals served their sentences, all three of their victims would be alive.

Wootton reports that statistics from the Bureau of Justice show that the median murder sentence is fifteen years but that murderers are out in five. The typical sentence for rape is eight years, but rapists are out in three. For robbery and assault, the typical sentences are six and four years, but the villains are out in two and one, respectively. The statistics show that 51 percent of violent criminals are out in two years or less and that 76 percent are out in three. More than 60 percent of released violent offenders are rearrested within three years for a serious crime. Judges hand down tough sentences just to mollify and deceive us, and behind closed doors, criminals are secretly turned loose on us.

Now all the talk is about hiring more police. What good is that? It's like bailing water out of a boat with a bucket that has holes in it. Seeing the foolhardiness of the effort, people call for bigger and more expensive buckets with holes in them. The boat is going to sink. Wootton says that by requiring criminals to serve at least 85 percent of their sentenced time, we could prevent 4,400,000 violent crimes, nearly three-quarters of the total violent crimes committed each year.

You say, "Williams, where are we going to put the criminals if we take your lock'em-up-and-throw-away-the-key approach? The jails are overcrowded now!" No problem. There are U.S. trust territories in the Pacific Ocean. We can build cinder-block containers and let the sharks be the guards.

The bottom line is that if there is one basic legitimate function of government, it is to protect its citizens against predators. Politicians have failed miserably in this basic job, and to make matters worse, they now want to take guns away from law-abiding citizens, thereby making us sitting ducks for criminals. But if you think about it, politicians and criminals have a lot in common. Both are in the business of taking what belongs to us.

Rights to Self-Defense

AUGUST 31, 1994

Let's think through the continuing attack on our constitutional protection to keep and bear arms. Try to find a flaw in the impeccable logic that follows. The fundamental starting point is that we each own ourselves. If we own ourselves, we have the right to protect ourselves against those who would violate self-ownership through aggressive acts like murder, rape, or theft. Historically, private acts of aggression pale in comparison to government-sponsored or -sanctioned aggression, such as slavery, extermination, purges, and imperialism.

This brutal lesson of history was not forgotten by our founders. Thomas Jefferson observed, "When governments fear the people, there is liberty. When the people fear the government, there is tyranny." He added, "The strongest reason for the people to retain the right to keep and bear arms is, as a last resort, to protect themselves against tyranny in government."

Increasingly, Americans are coming to fear their government. We fear the Internal Revenue Service (IRS), whom Congress has given the power to invade our privacy and require us to obey regulations that neither it nor anyone else understands. Not long ago, an official of the increasingly terrorist Environmental Protection Agency (EPA) said he longed for the day when a call from the EPA would instill as much fear in citizens as a call from the IRS. Then there's the increasing fear of the gestapolike tactics of the Bureau of Alcohol, Tobacco and Firearms, the Fish and Wildlife Service, the Food and Drug Administration, the

Drug Enforcement Agency, and the Corps of Engineers. Congress sanctions these agencies to summarily violate major elements of our Bill of Rights guarantees, and a derelict Supreme Court sits in silence or complicity.

George Mason could have just as easily been talking about today's antigun movement when he said, "To disarm the people is the best and most effectual way to enslave them." And who's behind this movement? It's for the most part liberals in and out of Congress who want to make us servants of the state. They're the educationists who want to propagandize our children, the environmental extremists who'd like to trespass on our property with impunity, and the wicked busybodies in and out of government.

They try to exploit our constitutional ignorance by claiming the Second Amendment refers to a "well-regulated militia" and government does the regulating. Nonsense! Noah Webster defined militia as "the effective part of the people at large," and George Mason defined militia as "the whole people, except for a few public officials." The framers knew that government at the very best was a "necessary evil" but that its central tendency was to become an intolerable evil. The Second Amendment was written to give us a fighting chance. With pious expressions, liberals often ask, "Why would anybody want a military assault weapon? You can't hunt with it." They want us to believe that the framers gave us the Second Amendment so that we could hunt deer and duck and do a little target practice.

Before we surrender our guns, we should remember that history's most barbaric people were also gun-ban advocates. Adolf Hitler sought a strict ban on gun possession by Jews. All over the post–Civil War South, laws were written to restrict the sale of guns to blacks. Hitler and Southern racists weren't trying to fight crime. They sought to prevent Jews and blacks from defending themselves. Of course, the legislation didn't say that. In fact, I know of no evil legislation written in explicitly evil language, including the Brady bill.

So far as crime is concerned, we should enforce existing laws and put criminals away. But I bet that if more law-abiding citizens carried guns, there'd be less street crime. Criminals are cowards and prey on the defenseless.

Clinton's Crime Bill

AUGUST 17, 1994

It's getting harder to deal pure pork, so Clinton and Congress must do some sleight of hand, and this time, it's the crime bill. But the fight to enact it reveals another sorry saga about racial problems. Clinton blamed the National Rifle Association and the Republicans for the crime bill's earlier eight-vote defeat in the House, and the media sang the same tune. However, the president could have just as easily blamed the eleven congressional Black Caucus members who voted no because the bill didn't contain their "Racial Justice Act." But blaming black congressmen isn't politically correct.

The Racial Justice Act would prohibit "the imposition or execution of the death penalty in a racially discriminatory pattern" and lead to execution quotas. There is no question the death penalty has historically been imposed in a racially discriminatory manner. In 1848, for example, Virginia enacted a statute mandating that blacks be executed for a crime for which a white person might receive a three-year jail sentence. Other evidence shows gross death sentence discrimination, particularly in the South before the 1950s.

Writing in *Public Interest* (summer 1994), Stanley Rothman and Stephen Powers report that all that has changed. In their article "Execution by Quota?" they conclude that if the death sentence controversy were weighted on merits of research, we'd all have to concede "that death penalty discrimination has been virtually eliminated."

Those who claim discrimination cite evidence that blacks are more likely to receive a death sentence for murdering a white than for murdering a black. According to a study of three southern states, only 64 percent of blacks who murdered blacks were executed whereas 81 percent of those murdering whites were put to death. A Georgia study reports that 11 percent of blacks who killed whites were put to death whereas just 1 percent of blacks who killed blacks got the same sentence.

At first blush, this looks like discrimination, but we have to look further. First, murder is not integrated. About 97 percent of homicides are intraracial. Most black-on-black murders result from a dispute between people who know each other. However, black-on-white murders frequently involve armed robbery, rape, beatings, and kidnapping. In Georgia, that was true in 67 percent of black-on-white cases, compared with only 7 percent of black-on-black cases.

Courts are more likely to impose the death sentence when there are aggravating circumstances (rape, robbery, and beatings). Therefore, given this reality, we shouldn't be surprised by the racial outcome. Moreover, death sentences are especially likely when the case involves killing a police officer in the line of duty, and 85 percent of police officers killed are white. So even if the same number of blacks and whites killed policemen, the odds are strongly in favor of a black's victim being a white officer. Rothman and Powers conclude, "The best available evidence indicates that disproportionate numbers of blacks commit murder, and that in those cases in which the victims are white, the crimes are aggravated. That is why blacks are over-represented on death row." Bureau of Justice statistics may be interpreted to suggest greater leniency toward blacks because the percentage of blacks on death row is 42 percent whereas the number charged with murder is 48 percent.

Homicide is a devastating problem for black neighborhoods. It's the number one cause of death of young men. That's a problem that won't be solved by charlatans in the Black Caucus peddling the Racial Justice Act. White liberals are crazier and more demeaning than I estimated for lending support.

We've Had Enough

OCTOBER 25, 1994

"America does not have a crime problem; inner-city America does." That's what Princeton professor of political science John J. DiIulio says, and he's just about right. If we ignored inner-city violent crime, mostly committed by blacks and Hispanics, America would be a fairly civilized place. "Damn it, there you go again, Williams," you say, "giving aid and comfort to America's racists." Let's look at it.

Professor DiIulio's article, "The Question of Black Crime," appearing in *Public Interest* (fall 1994), reports that blacks are 20 percent of the general population of the nation's seventy-five most populous urban counties. However, blacks were 54 percent of murder victims and 62 percent of all murder defendants. In Washington, D.C., between 1985 and 1988, three-quarters of all murders were by blacks against blacks. In Pennsylvania, 42 percent of the state's violent crimes takes place in Philadelphia, which contains only 14 percent of the state's population, most of them occurring in several predominantly black neighborhoods. In 1990, nearly 49 percent of state prisoners and 31 percent of federal prisoners were black. Compared with white prisoners, they were more likely to have committed a violent crime.

These new dismal statistics lead us to ask why. In 1960, there were 783 people in prison for every 1,000 violent crimes. By 1980, it was 227 per 1,000 violent crimes, a drop of 69 percent. Nationally, within three years of sentencing and while on probation, about half of all probationers are arrested for a new crime or abscond. About three-quarters of all convicted criminals are not incarcerated. Where are they? Callous courts, prosecutors, and parole boards have set them free to prey on and "imprison" law-abiding citizens.

The victims of liberal harebrained schemes on how to treat criminals are mostly poor blacks and Hispanics. They can't afford to move to a safer environment, and police do not protect them. Boston University professor Glenn Loury, pointing to the murder of Polly Klaas by a violent repeat criminal, suggests there is a muting of outrage in the black community: "If the degree of energy and organizational skill invested in campaigns against racially motivated violence, or against police brutality, or against the death penalty, were instead expended voicing demands that bad men be kept behind bars, these demands would become irresistible." Black ambivalence toward and identification with black criminals explains the difference between the celebrity status of Polly Klaas and the anonymity of countless young black victims.

When we talk about jailing predators, liberals come up with the lame lament that it costs $25,000 to keep a criminal in jail and less than that to send him to college. They want us to believe that predators would attend college if only they had the chance. But jailing criminals is a bargain. DiIulio reports that in 1992 crime victims lost $17.2

billion in direct costs. That doesn't include medical costs, pain and suffering, fear, and prevention measures.

There's no denying that poor law-abiding blacks and Hispanics are overwhelmingly the primary victims of crime. They live in fear and terror. They are the people whose neighborhoods have been turned into mini-Beiruts. Politicians and liberals, who live on the outskirts of town, respond to their plight by searching for "original causes" and proposals for midnight basketball. Blacks and Hispanics must ignore the criminal nonsense of their "leaders" and elected officials and say, "We've had enough and we're not going to take it anymore!"

Civilized People versus Barbarians

FEBRUARY 24, 1993

The essence of human history is the ongoing struggle between barbarians and civilized people. You say, "I might go along with that, but what's your definition of a barbarian?" It's easy. In principle, barbarians are people who have little respect for private property, whereas civilized people honor and respect private property. That's why theft qualifies as a barbaric act. Because we own ourselves, rape and murder are also barbaric because they violate private property.

People are not born civilized. On the contrary, they are born barbarians, caring little for the rights and property of others. The role of the family is to civilize these imps before we set them loose on society, a challenging job as any mother and father will tell you. But parents alone cannot do the complete job; it requires other inputs that we call institutions, community, and values.

Let's look at what's been happening. When I was a child, during the 1940s, the "vexing" problems teachers and principals faced were chewing gum, talking in line, passing notes in class, and going up the down stairs. Compare that with today's school problems of knives and guns, rape, murder, and serious assaults by students on teachers and other students. There are two reasons for this. First, we've undermined civilizing authority through laws inhibiting strict discipline. Just as important, there has been a decline in the teaching of moral absolutes and a rise in the worship of moral relativism—if it feels good, do it. Because the Bible deals with moral absolutes, liberals are hostile to any biblical influence in schools.

But it's not only Bible lessons that are rejected by today's liberals. They reject the moral absolutes found in the childhood stories I read such as "The Little Red Hen," "The Ant and the Grasshopper," "The Tortoise and the Hare," and Aesop's *Fables*. Those stories taught the moral superiority of hard work, thrift, and perseverance. Liberals probably condemn the little red hen, who wouldn't share her bread with the barnyard bums, as a racist or a selfish Reaganite. They'd probably say that those barnyard bums had an "entitlement" to the fruit of the hen's toil.

In the lexicon of barbarians, no word is as important as entitlement. It covers up the violation of private property for those too squeamish to face facts. An ordinary thief thinks he's entitled to your property and takes it. However, such direct action risks imprisonment. The more prudent tactic is to convince a congressman that you are entitled to the property of others, and he'll use his paid henchmen to get it for you. That way, you're just a recipient of stolen property rather than a thief but nonetheless a barbarian for your disregard for private property.

Looked at this way, most of our nation's problems are a result of barbarism. The founders of this nation appreciated this. Benjamin Franklin said, "When the people find they can vote themselves money, that will herald the end of the republic." Our Constitution promotes moral absolutes. Its strict interpretation would mean that two-thirds of the federal budget and most federal activity would be found unconstitutional. That, by the way, is why U.S. Supreme Court nominees who are seen as strict constructionists are pilloried by liberals, the news media, and many congressmen. Can you imagine what would have happened to Clarence Thomas had he suggested there was no constitutional authority for most of what government does?

At times, being a civilized person is too costly, and I think about joining America's barbarians.

Military Ineffectiveness

MARCH 24, 1993

Measures are being taken that will weaken our military effectiveness. First, there's the push to lift the Pentagon ban on homosexuals. By the way, if the ban is lifted, shouldn't homosexuals be housed separately for the same reasons women are? The bigger problem is the call to lift the ban on women in combat.

William S. Lind, former defense adviser to Senator Gary Hart, says the nondeployability rate for women during the gulf war was four times higher than for men, primarily due to a 10 to 14 percent pregnancy rate.

Then there's *gender norming*, similar to the race norming practiced by the U.S. Department of Labor. When men and women do identical exercises, women's scores are weighted to compensate for their physical deficiencies. At West Point, there's no more training in combat boots because women experience high rates of injury. Running with heavy weapons has been eliminated to accommodate the physical weakness of women. Obstacle course events requiring upper-body strength have been eliminated. If women are allowed in combat, we should push for changes in the rules of engagement so that our enemies accommodate our social commitment.

David Horowitz, author of *The Feminist Assault on the Military*, says there's a pattern of information suppression on female deficiencies in traditionally male jobs. Some policemen, off the record, tell of dangers they face because of women partners who are not as physically intimidating as men. Construction workers tell of having to carry women forced onto their crews who are not strong enough to do heavy work.

Women should have opportunities to compete with men. However, equality before the law does not require or imply that men and women are equal in all respects. Indeed, according to studies conducted at West Point, there are 120 physical differences between men and women that may bear on military requirements. That information, and its consequences for military preparedness, is suppressed. The official position put forward by Patricia Schroeder (D-Colo.), Barbara Mikulski (D-Md.), and Rear Admiral Virgil Hill is to call for the "immediate dismissal of senior officers who question the role of women in the military."

Advocates of combat roles for women frequently point to Israel's use of women. Israelis did use women in combat but now bar them. Horowitz says the Israelis found that "if you put women in combat with men, the men immediately forget about their tactical objective, and they move instead to protect the women." You say, "Williams, that's not the fault of women; it's a weakness of men." You might be right. Schroeder and her feminist allies have a plan. The air force has established a survival, evasion, resistance, and escape program to desensitize male recruits so they won't act like men when female prisoners of war are tortured.

Then there's the question about the psychological stamina of women. A three-star admiral lost a promotion because the newsletter for which he was responsible printed this joke: "Beer is better than women because beer never has a headache." Three top-gun fliers were relieved of their command because they witnessed or participated in a skit lampooning Schroeder. These acts may be tasteless, but if feminine feelings are that fragile, how can we expect women to have the stomach to kill, maim, and destroy? An enemy could have them sobbing on the battlefield simply by broadcasting sexist jokes.

Traditional Values

APRIL 7, 1993

No matter how you cut it, our most serious national problems stem from an abandonment of traditional standards of morality. Despite what the liberal elite would have us believe, there are moral absolutes and there's right and wrong. Some behavior is good, and some is wicked. Whether you're a Christian, Jew, or atheist, certain behaviors are to be encouraged, while others are to be scorned and condemned. Let's look at it.

Traditionally, we've condemned both teenage sex and bearing children without the benefit of marriage. There's good reason. Teenagers have neither the means nor the maturity to raise children. Liberal values that comfort and sanction bastardy have produced disastrous results. The poverty rate of traditional, two-parent, intact families is one-sixth that of nontraditional families. In nontraditional families, child abuse is forty times higher and children are three times as likely to have emotional and behavioral problems.

Congress plays a major role in the breakup of the traditional family. For most of our history, the average father's earnings provided for the family because the average earner paid little or no taxes. Now, because of federal and state income taxes, Social Security, and property taxes, a man earning $30,000 a year has an after-tax income of a bit over $20,000. This tax bite forces some wives into abandoning young ones just to make ends meet. All of this was done by stealth. Had the 1945 income tax deduction for children kept pace with congressionally caused inflation, the average worker would pay little or no income taxes.

Government schools have also contributed to undermining traditional values. Whether it's a decline in discipline, a fall in standards, or bait-and-switch sex education programs teaching youngsters that anything goes provided you start out with a condom, our schools have led the way in undermining traditional values. If you pay $23,000 and your kid goes on to elite universities like Stanford, he may have access to "Safe Sex Explorer's Action-Packed Starter Kit Handbook," a manual that advises, "Mutual masturbation is great—but watch out for cuts on hands and raw genitals. . . . Use condoms for f———g with several partners. Always clean up and change rubbers before going from one person to another."

There are good reasons why the elite and the liberal press attack what they derisively call the religious right and the "Ozzie and Harriet" family. They attack religion for the identical reason the communists attack it: Religion is about moral absolutes. There is no equivocation about its routine condemnation of fornication, adultery, homosexuality, stealing, lying, and cheating. Religion says children should be loyal to and obedient to parents. Parents have a responsibility to their children. Bums, derelicts, and hobos have become our society's mascots, but religion has always condemned slothful behavior.

Pretend you're a liberal whose agenda calls for people's allegiance to be first and foremost to government. You want open sex and any kind of lifestyle. You want a nanny government that confiscates the earnings of one American and gives them to another to whom they do not belong. What institutions challenge your agenda and stand in your way? You've got it: families and religion.

Even our financial problems like federal deficit and debt are rooted in immorality. After all, thrift, deferred gratification, and living within one's means are moral values as well. To revitalize our nation, we don't need more of Washington's wicked agenda. We need a moral reawakening.

It's Really a Matter of Morality

OCTOBER 6, 1993

While Americans wail about this or that aspect of Congress's recently enacted, largest tax increase in our history, let's come to grips with this fact: Our fiscal problems stem from a long, relentless retreat from the moral principles established by our Constitution.

Social or entitlement spending accounts for the bulk of runaway spending and the resulting deficits and debts over the last several decades. Crop, welfare, and business handouts are little more than congressionally imposed obligations on one set of citizens for the benefit of another. I challenge any congressman to demonstrate federal government's constitutional or moral authority for using its coercive power this way.

The church, legal scholars, the occasional politician, and a sense of do right by citizens at large used to be our moral anchor. These people, values, and institutions that once served us well are today either ignorant or contemptuous of our Constitution. Without a moral anchor, we're adrift in a sea of immorality, headed toward economic and social chaos. Our law schools are little more than dens of iniquity that nurture and breed the constitutional derelicts we have in Congress, before the bar, and on the bench. Ask a lawyer what's the constitutional authority for government's imposing obligations on some to provide what has become known as entitlements for others. You'll get grossly ignorant answers ranging from it's in the Constitution to promote the general welfare to it's the government's responsibility. If that lawyer graduated from one of our more prestigious schools, he'll lecture you that the Constitution was written when times were simpler. It's a "living document" adaptable to the complexities of today.

Balderdash! A constitution establishes "rules of the game," standards of conduct among people and their government. For game rules to have meaning and usefulness and be just, they can't be "living." How would you like to play poker with me? There you sit with three of a kind, and I tell you my pair of aces wins because Hoyle's rules, our poker constitution, have been adapted to the complexities of my life.

Established churches are equally contemptuous of constitutional and moral principles. Ministers and bishops descend on congressional offices to lobby for this or that social spending agenda. They differ little from other Washington hustlers who beg and promise constituent votes as a means to persuade congressmen to use the power of their office to confiscate that which rightfully belongs to one American and give it to those the ministers think should have it.

While your bishop or minister may support government welfare, food-stamp and housing programs, ask him whether he supports the methods whereby government obtains the resources. More specifically, ask him whether he can show the Christian basis for using force to take what belongs to one person to give to another. If it's OK in his book for government to do it, ask him what does he think of it being done privately. The latter is called theft. Although your minister won't come out and say it, he probably believes that the commandment Thou Shalt Not Steal only applies to private acts. But if there's a majority vote, and it's done by government, it's no longer theft in the eyes of God but charity. How morally shallow can one be?

Widespread retreat from morality is the bad news. The good news is Americans have never done wrong things for a long time. We tend to come to our senses and try to set things right. I hope I live to see it.

Social Parasites versus Us

NOVEMBER 17, 1993

The murder of Michael Jordan's father is just more evidence of a reluctance to defend ourselves from social scum. Jordan's dad is dead because of a liberal-designed justice system that places the interests of criminals before those of law-abiding citizens. Thus, it was possible for two lawless and violent punks, who should have been in prison, to be free to commit mayhem and murder.

If we really think about it, the liberal agenda has us paying all kinds of costs for social parasites. As a result of our tolerance for holdups, we bear the inconvenience of needing exact change to use public transportation. Poor people must travel long distances to do ordinary shopping because criminals have turned their neighborhoods into economic wastelands. We're forced to spend billions on items like the Club, burglar alarms, and steel window bars and doors to protect our persons and valuables.

Instead of building more jails, arresting social predators, and imprisoning them, authorities teach us not to resist holdups and rape. Don't carry much cash, they say. Lock valuables in the trunk of your car, and lock your car door. Don't jog alone in parks. Establish neighborhood watches. What authorities don't tell us is why we're paying for them to protect us if we must protect ourselves. Liberals preach the poppycock that crime would be reduced by passing laws making gun ownership more difficult for law-abiding citizens.

Along with a reluctance to protect ourselves from social parasites, we give them a free hand to attack what's decent about us. The Boy Scouts of America is a decent organization. It is one of America's strongest forces for building moral character among young men. Plus, its members do yeomanlike volunteer work. Recently, the 5.5 million-member organization has come under scurrilous attack because of its stance against sodomy and its unwillingness to admit homosexual scoutmasters.

In 1992, because of the Boy Scouts' exclusion of homosexuals, Levi Strauss Company, Bank of America, Wells Fargo, and United Way yanked donations. That's great. We idly sit by while a group trying to spread

decency, honesty, and American values is penalized. Then we heap
money and compassion on people whose behavior and advocacy spread
the most deadly disease known to mankind, not to mention creating an
astronomical burden on our health care system.

Boy Scouts aren't the only decent group under liberal-led siege. The
U.S. Senate recently denied its congressionally protected reauthoriza-
tion of the design patent for the insignia of the United Daughters of the
Confederacy (UDC). Illinois senator Carol Moseley-Braun whined that
the UDC insignia (stars in a field of stripes) is a stark reminder of slavery. United Daughters of the Confederacy consists of twenty-four thousand southern ladies who do volunteer work at Veterans Administration hospitals and, over the years, have awarded thousands of scholar-
ships. After the Moseley-Braun Senate temper tantrum, seventy-five
spineless, mammy-whipped senators voted no on the patent reauthori-
zation.

But months earlier, the same senators voted to confirm homosexual
activist Roberta Achtenberg as Clinton's assistant secretary for Fair
Housing and Equal Opportunity. While a San Francisco supervisor, Achtenberg led the attack on the Boy Scouts. That's our pattern: punish or
not defend decency and reward and fund those who attack decency.

Decent Americans must get serious quickly about defending what
forces for decency remain. A good start is to stop giving our money to
charitable organizations and to refuse to patronize businesses that allow themselves to be used in the attack on decency.

Trashing Traditional Values

JANUARY 12, 1993

How come men don't whimper and wail when insulted by foul language and rude behavior? We just return the favor in kind, and, if the
situation calls for it, we have a fair one—rumble. Even if you can't
rumble, you don't whimper and wail. That's for sissies—at least traditionally. Also, traditionally, behavior acceptable among men was not
acceptable between men and women. Thankfully, there was a double

standard. Women could say and do things, such as slap your face, that wouldn't be tolerated if done by a man. Boys were indoctrinated to treat women differently. This made sense because, given enormous male and female strength differences, women would always come out on the short end of the rumble.

For the last several decades, we've been told that women are equal to men, that we must eliminate double standards, that there must be liberation. We've seen the effects of that message. Some men make lewd comments to women and treat them in a manner that not even the lowest of lowlifes would have fifty years ago. And we're all naively surprised. While we were trashing spontaneously evolved traditional values for male/female relationships, we forgot their purposes. Instead of recognizing the folly and recapturing those values, like fools, we think government sex harassment laws are suitable substitutes.

Our attack on traditional values runs deep. During the past several decades, there has been a successful attack on all centers of authority except government. For example, what's the appropriate decision-making unit for whether a teenage girl has an abortion? You'd think parents were. Now, that decision often lies in the hands of a judge or social welfare agency. What's worse, the decision is often made with neither the knowledge nor the consent of parents. Hillary Clinton has long advocated the right of children to sue and "divorce" parents, using taxpayer funds to do so. With traditional family authority having been undermined, should we be surprised to see so many of our children rebel against, curse, and even assault their parents?

Look at all the flap over Clinton's marital infidelity, pot smoking, draft dodging, and other moral indiscretions. The fact that Clinton is what he is doesn't say much. His faults are shared by millions of men. As such, it's nothing new. What's new is that at no time in our history could a man who was a known draft dodger, flagrant womanizer, and pot smoker be elected to the nation's highest office. This is the first time in our history where military men, from top brass on down, have to be ordered and lectured to respect the commander in chief. The fact that Clinton is the president of the United States says little about Clinton but a lot about widespread national moral degeneration.

There are many other indications of moral capitulation and degeneration. We allow our children to bring home vulgar music that our parents would never have allowed. Instead of parents setting limits, we call for Congress to regulate the entertainment industry. We explain away wicked behavior of murderers, rapists, and social parasites by calling them "sick" or saying society made them do it. We give top billing to afternoon TV talk shows that feature grossly deviant behavior. It's one thing to be tolerant of private deviant behavior. It's quite another to accept it as morally equivalent and normal. People have children they can't afford. Instead of holding them accountable, we make others accountable through the tax code.

Unless Americans summon the courage to confront the liberal/leftist government-backed assault on tradition, values, and accountability, we are going to bequeath to future generations a demoralized, decayed nation.

Bad News That's Good, Kinda

JANUARY 5, 1993

Charles Murray, American Enterprise Institute scholar and author of *Losing Ground* (Basic Books, 1994), wrote a thoughtful *Wall Street Journal* article "The Coming White Underclass," published October 29, 1993. Like Daniel Patrick Moynihan, who in the 1960s sounded the alarm about growing illegitimacy—at that time 26 percent—and the breakdown of the black family, Murray has sounded the same alarm about white illegitimacy. The overall illegitimacy rate among whites is 22 percent and growing. Eighty-two percent of that illegitimacy is among women with a high school education or less.

We're all well aware of black illegitimacy, which now stands at 68 percent and in some cities is over 80 percent. Back in the 1960s, had someone predicted today's rate of black illegitimacy, he would have been judged insane or a racist. Is anyone foolhardy enough to say what happened to blacks cannot happen to whites? White people aren't any more immune to the breakdown in family values and the devastating effects of welfarism than blacks.

Murray says, "Illegitimacy is the single most important social problem of our time—more important than crime, drugs, poverty, illiteracy, welfare or homelessness because it drives everything else." In other words, illegitimacy either is a major cause of those problems or exacerbates them. Murray adds that concentrated large numbers of boys growing up without fathers creates a culture equivalent to that in the *Lord of the Flies,* where the unsocialized values of male adolescents become the norm—violence, instant gratification, and predatory sex. That, Murray argues, is precisely the culture taking over the black inner city.

Today's welfarism is entirely new. It's a system championed by airheaded liberals and politicians all too ready to tax and spend. Liberal elites like Professor Andrew Cherlin, a Johns Hopkins University sociologist, teach it has yet to be shown that the "absence of a father was directly responsible for any of the supposed deficiencies of broken homes." According to Cherlin and his crowd, the problem "is not the lack of male presence but the lack of male income." Fathers can be replaced by a welfare check.

Marriage is paramount. Charles Murray says we must restore the penalties for having children outside of marriage by ending all economic support for single mothers. Single mothers would have to do what they used to do if they want to keep the child: enlist support from parents, boyfriends, siblings, neighbors, churches, and philanthropies. Doing this would get mature adults involved with the raising of the child, teach the girl responsibility, and renew the social stigma to illegitimacy. The alternative to keeping the baby is adoption, and, Murray says, "We should spend lavishly on orphanages."

To increase the rewards of marriage, we should change the tax code so that it stops penalizing marriage and children. We should make marriage the sole legal institution through which parental rights and responsibilities are defined and exercised.

If there is any good news about the rise in white illegitimacy and welfarism, it's that we can finally take the issue out of the racial arena and treat it as a human problem. I have always said welfare has done to black families what slavery, reconstruction, and the rawest racism could not have done. And what's happening to whites is proof that the welfare cancer has nothing to do with genetics.

Everybody's a Victim

JULY 6, 1994

Let's talk about victims and victimhood. We all know that blacks suffer from racism and the legacy of slavery. Therefore, government programs promoting differential treatment and societal double standards are a must for justice. The fact that blacks have higher unemployment, are less likely to have a college education, have a shorter life expectancy, and are more likely to be in jail is unambiguous evidence of unreconstructed white exploitation.

But maybe the reason white people exploit black people is because they've been exploited by Asian Americans. White people have higher unemployment, lower income, and less education and are more likely to be in jail than Asian Americans. And to top off that kind of oppression, Asian Americans, while receiving less prenatal care, have lower infant mortality rates than whites. Even Hispanics have lower infant mortality rates than whites. Then, to add insult to injury, bankers turn down whites for home mortgages at a greater rate than they do Asian Americans.

That's only the beginning of white Anglo-Saxon suffering. Back in 1066, white people in England were living the life of Riley—out on the beach, downing brews, and chasing the ladies. Then in came the Normans, French white people, pillaging their towns, raping their women, and trying to make them speak French. However, if you think about it, those whites got what they deserved but in reverse. As soon as Britishers regained their strength, they started exploiting the people of Ireland, trying to make them Protestants.

Every once in a while, you hear Italians complain about discrimination. But they have no legitimate gripe. Look at how Italians exploited Ethiopia and backed fascism in Spain. From a historical justice point of view, forgetting about Mussolini, Italians are getting off easy.

Ignoring the conquest of Canaan, which doesn't count since it was before Christ, Jews are the only people who can lay claim to being a pure victim class. It's just that they've done so well everywhere they've gone, except Israel, they give the appearance of ripping people off.

Women are double victims, once racially and then sexually. Women are 52 percent of the population, but they are 0 percent of professional football and basketball players. I've yet to turn on the television and see a woman boxing. But whatever discrimination they face is probably deserved because they're not very fair with men. Women own about 70 percent of the nation's wealth and live 10 to 15 percent longer than men. If there were true sex equality, wealth would be distributed nearly fifty-fifty, and men would live as long as women. Congress can deal with the wealth inequality, but what could it do about the life span inequality? Because Congress doesn't have the power to make men live longer, I shudder at the thought of its other justice alternative.

Racism and sexism bother me, but it's heightism that really gets me. God has blessed me with a superior physical endowment: I'm nearly 6 feet 6 inches tall. Social jealousy has created gross societal discrimination and insensitivity to my height. There are all sorts of laws making life easier for victims of age and ability, not to mention victims of winks and whistles. But what about height discrimination victims? Water fountains force me to choose between breaking my back and dehydration. Then there are the low urinals and short airplane seats. Clothing stores either don't carry my size or charge me more than people of diminutive stature.

Without a doubt, we're a nation of victims. But how come some victims get government programs while others are routinely ignored or victimized even more?

Sowing Seeds of Destruction

SEPTEMBER 21, 1994

The ethnic, regional, language, and religious conflicts we've seen in Bosnia, Rwanda, Ireland, Quebec, and numerous other places didn't crop up overnight. They resulted from decades, sometimes centuries, of one group of people using government force to impose their values, ways, and visions of a good life on others. While we've made some mistakes here in the United States, there's been nothing like the ethnic, language, and religious barbarism witnessed elsewhere.

It would seem that we'd be a plausible candidate for ethnic, language, and religious violence. After all, Americans represent virtually every ethnic, language, and religious group in the world. Despite that fact, people who for centuries have been trying to slaughter each other in their homelands came here and somehow managed to live together with a fair amount of harmony and cooperation.

However, with this harmony and cooperation, there's been one major blemish—our bloody, brutal Civil War. While many history books portray the war as a battle to eliminate slavery, it was more a war of regional interests, grievances, and conflict. But let's not debate that. Just suffice it to say that Americans are not immune from what turns out to be the most brutal of conflicts—fratricidal wars.

If a Hutu or Tutsi, a Croat or Serb, or a Protestant or Irish Catholic participant in random slaughter were asked what was the original grievance causing the hate and violence, I doubt whether a reasonably accurate or intelligent answer could be given. But most likely, the causes can be summarized as one group of people using government to win special favors and forcibly impose their values and preferences on another.

Civility is fragile, and civil societies can become uncivil. The seeds of incivility are rapidly being sown in many ways in our country. Just recently, Representative Vic Fazio jumped on conservative Christians. His attack was followed up by Clinton's on the Reverends Jerry Falwell and Pat Robertson, alleging they'd crossed the line of decency. For their part, conservative Christians have maintained a constant attack on Clinton and the policies of his administration.

But the Reverends Falwell and Robertson's attacks on Clinton and other liberals are predictable. You don't have to be an evangelical Christian, crossing the line of decency, to object to and be offended by government distribution of condoms to your kid when you teach him chastity. Many people find abortion offensive, but insult is added to injury when government takes their earnings to support it. There are people who find pornography ungodly but can tolerate those who enjoy it. The best way to make them intolerant is to take their earnings to finance it. Many Christians condemn homosexuality as an abomination in the eyes of God, but they can civilly tolerate those who choose that lifestyle. How do you make them intolerant? It's easy. Use government schools and taxpayer money to teach such a person's child that homosexuality and heterosexuality are morally equivalent.

Unfortunately, President Clinton and his administration bigwigs like Joycelyn Elders and Donna Shalala are strong supporters of ideas and practices that conservative Christians and many other Americans find both offensive and overly intrusive. For right now, it's just hot words, but grievances that erupt into widescale bloody, brutal conflict always start out with hot words. And once it moves beyond hot words, it has a sustaining mind of its own.

We've been sowing seeds of incivility for decades, so President Clinton can't be held totally accountable. But we'd better quickly reverse course and recognize that multireligious and multiethnic societies are fragile at best and can blow up in our faces.

Giving Up

November 16, 1994

No doubt this is going to come as a shock to those who've seen me as courage personified and America's beacon of hope. I'm tired, misused, abused, and finally giving up and claiming victim's status like everyone else. I am a multifaceted victim of societal injustice. Don't jump to conclusions. My victimization isn't a result of my three hundred years of suffering under the yoke of slavery followed by Jim Crowism and rankest racism. I've already forgiven white people, Arabs, and my African ancestors for selling me into slavery. It's not even those infamous last twelve years where Reagan and Bush stopped taxing the rich and put the entire tax burden on the backs of the poor.

It's those little abuses, insensitivities, and inconsiderations that get me. According to my tax records, not only does Congress force me to pay for my share of the missiles, but I have to clothe, house, and feed at least three American families. That bothers me some, but what really gets me is that I can't claim tax deductions for my extended family— and they don't even have the courtesy to send me a Father's Day card or a thank-you note.

Then there's gross societal insensitivity to my height. Through no fault of my own, I am nearly 6 feet 6 inches tall. Congress has passed all sorts of laws making life easier for age victims, crippled people, victims of winks and whistles, and nonsmokers, but what about victims of height? We face callous indifference. Some water fountains are so low, I'm forced to choose between straining my back and dehydration. Then there are the low urinals and cramped airplane seats. The Americans with Disabilities Act should be amended to mandate higher fountains and urinals and tall people's sections on airplanes.

There's another problem people of diminutive stature never encounter: clothing store insensitivity. I've gone to hundreds of clothing and shoe stores' sales. I get there, and most often my size is unavailable. If it is available, they gouge me by charging a higher price. Height is an uncontrollable physical attribute just like race and sex. There'd be all sorts of Equal Employment Opportunity Commission hell if clothing stores charged a Mexican or a woman a higher price. Salesmen try to fool me by saying it isn't heightism but the cost of extra material. Nonsense! They don't charge fat people more.

The only official racism left in America is Social Security racism. Black male life expectancy at birth is 64.2 years. Congress takes just as much Social Security tax out of my paycheck as it does out of the paycheck of a white guy who has a life expectancy of 73.0 years. Then it tells me I can't get full benefits until age sixty-five. It's a racial rip-off; they know that I'm going to croak eight months before eligibility starts and that the white guy is going to get at least eight years or so of benefits. Being a sensitive person, I am not calling for Congress to make white guys live only as long as I.

Instead of the Black Caucus fretting over whether the Confederate flag flies in Georgia and urging President Clinton to make Haiti streets as safe as those in Detroit, Los Angeles, and Washington, D.C., it should lead the fight to "race norm" Social Security. Because white guys average eight years of drawing Social Security checks, what's wrong with blacks averaging eight years too? In order to have Social Security justice, the act should be amended so that black males are eligible for Social Security payments starting at age fifty-six. That way, we'd get eight years of benefit checks too.

Things That Sound Good

NOVEMBER 30, 1994

At the heart of much of what's wrong in America is the decades-long process of replacing things that worked with what sounds good. Take arithmetic. During the early 1940s, when I was in elementary school, we learned our numbers by rote. The teacher would call on different students to recite parts of the multiplication table. That kind of "oppression" was replaced by the new math. Its result: If stores didn't have cash registers that automatically compute the customer's change, they'd be out of business.

How about crime? When criminals were seen as wicked people, as opposed to sick, and we responded by punishing them and locking up habitual offenders (three-time losers) for life, there was less crime. But the psychobabblists convinced us to switch our emphasis from punishment to rehabilitation. As a result, criminals control the streets and law-abiding citizens must be ever watchful of their lives and property.

In the process of civilizing children, a well-justified spanking was seen as a valuable tool. Summers were the worst time for a spanking. Windows were open, and all of your playmates could hear you pleading, "I'll be good. I won't do it anymore." The next day, you'd face their taunts and ridicule. The psychobabblists got us again. We were told that children ought to be allowed to express themselves and that spanking is child abuse. Now many children have no reservations about using the foulest of language to adults; often that adult is the parent. In a fashion, my mother went along with that expression business. We had expression sessions: I expressed myself, and she picked up a strap and expressed herself.

How about welfare? In the North Philadelphia housing project where I grew up, most were poor. But just about all of my neighborhood playmates lived with two parents with either one or both working. Today's Richard Allen project is different. Most kids live in female-headed households. Instead of work, welfare has become the way of life. Years ago, being on welfare was considered a disgrace. Today, welfare has become a "right" somewhat like those guaranteed by our

Constitution. For many, employment is a trek down to the mailbox for a "paycheck." As a result, we've immunized many poor people to the traditional cure for poverty—opportunities and a robust expanding economy.

Few politicians have the courage to say that we've made many mistakes over the last several decades and that we have to return to the commonsense basics of our elders. Instead, they and the "experts" try to continue to convince us that it's external factors that explain the antisocial behavior so prevalent today rather than gross individual character flaws. But as Abraham Lincoln warned, "You can't fool all the people all the time." Increasing numbers of Americans are wising up to the fact that the liberals have sold us a rotten bill of goods.

Some of this recognition is seen in the popularity of calls for truth in sentencing, our increased willingness to build more prisons, and put criminals away for a longer time. Americans are developing increased resistance to educationist demands to dig deeper into our pocket to fund government schools. More are interested in school choice plans. There's building public resentment against people who choose laziness, excuses, and welfare as a way of life.

We don't have to become excessively punitive to restore some of the common sense of yesteryear. We simply must stop believing those half-baked theories that only academics can believe and understand and get back to practices that work.

POTPOURRI

A few columns defy categorization. They follow.

Liberty Loss Update

MARCH 18, 1992

Environmentalists are on the attack again. The January 1992 edition of the *Freeman* reports that Ron Liccardi of Keeseville, New York, planned to turn a portion of his ten-acre property into a golf driving range. But New York state officials intervened, declaring part of Liccardi's property wetlands and threatening fines or imprisonment or both. It made no difference to state officials that Liccardi's property became a wetland because of overflow from state-constructed drainage pipes. In Willsboro, New York, Jim Hemus's thirty-one-acre property is traversed by an eighty-foot-wide wetland (swamp). State officials denied him a permit to build access across his swamp to the rest of his land.

These are two among thousands of instances of how government bureaucrats are dictating how people's property shall be used. Just how much these bureaucrats, doing the bidding of environmentalists, can trample upon private property rights will soon be settled by the U.S. Supreme Court in *Lucas v. South Carolina Coastal Council*. In the wake of Hurricane Hugo, South Carolina lawmakers passed a Beachfront Management Act to prevent "unwise development." As a result, David

Lucas was prevented from building houses on his two beachfront lots worth $1.2 million. With a stroke of the pen, South Carolina lawmakers made Lucas's property worthless. The Pacific Legal Foundation, on behalf of David Lucas, has filed an amicus curiae brief arguing that the Fifth Amendment guarantees all persons protection from deprivation of property. If government wants to restrict a property owner's reasonable use of his property for public benefit, it must pay just compensation.

Environmentalists went bonkers simply because the U.S. Supreme Court agreed to hear the case. In the *Lucas* case, and many other instances, local and state governments have destroyed private property values in the name of public purpose without making just compensation to owners as mandated by the Fifth Amendment. Environmentalists love this; they want government to be able to ride roughshod over our rights at zero cost. They find it easier to convince legislators to destroy $1.2 million worth of property, as in the *Lucas* case, if it can be done without compensating owners. New York's environmentalists can more easily persuade the New York state government to trample on the property rights of people like Ron Liccardi and Jim Hemus when there's no cost for doing so. If legislators were forced to compensate owners for financial losses, they'd think twice about running roughshod over private property rights in the name of saving swamps, kangaroo rats, or some hooting owl.

Any jurist who believes in the strict enforcement of our Fifth Amendment guarantees is an enemy to environmental Nazis. That, in part, accounts for some of the hostility toward the Judge Clarence Thomas appointment to the U.S. Supreme Court. That's why Senator Joseph Biden contemptuously waved Professor Richard Epstein's book *Takings* in the air during the confirmation proceedings. He saw Thomas's view of the Fifth Amendment as similar to 1930s Supreme Court justices who ruled much of President Roosevelt's New Deal legislation to be unconstitutional infringements on private property rights. That, by the way, is why Roosevelt sought to pack the Court with justices who'd sanction Fifth Amendment violations.

The U.S. Supreme Court might rule, in *Lucas*, to protect our private property rights, but I'd suggest we arm ourselves. Ultimately, there's only one solution for environmental activists: induced trespass.

Wealth and Poverty

SEPTEMBER 2, 1992

More than anything else, wealth results from a state of mind and a set of values. Government is not a source of wealth. Governments, including ours, are essentially parasitic; they consume and dispose of wealth produced by private individuals. Of course, government can make some people wealthier but only by plundering someone else. If we are truly concerned about the welfare of our fellow man, both at home and abroad, we'd better pay greater attention to just what creates wealth.

Some believe national wealth depends on natural resources because we just happen to be rich and simultaneously blessed with bountiful natural resources. South America and Africa are also blessed with bountiful natural resources but are home to the world's most miserably poor people. In contrast, Great Britain, Hong Kong, Japan, Switzerland, and Taiwan are resource-poor but home to the world's more affluent people. Some will argue that Third World people are poor as a result of colonialism. Hogwash! The United States was a colony and so were Australia, Canada, and New Zealand; Hong Kong is still a colony. On the other hand, Ethiopia, Liberia, Nepal, and Tibet were never colonies but are home to the poorest of the world's poor.

We can't ever give a complete explanation for why some people and nations are wealthy while others are miserably poor, but we have a pretty good idea. At the individual level, we can all agree that being well off at least requires motivation, self-discipline, self-respect, honesty, and respect for others. All these wealth-enhancing attributes are for naught unless, at the societal level, there is freedom of exchange, inviolability of private property, sanctity of contracts, and protection of the right to earn. Tragically, these very institutions that permit the accumulation of wealth are a tyrant's first targets for takeover.

The role of private property is not understood well; thus, we fall prey to charlatans and quacks with hidden agendas. Private property creates a powerful inducement for people to voluntarily behave in socially responsible ways. For example, because my home is privately owned, I reap the complete benefit (a higher selling price) from taking good care of it and bear the complete cost (lower selling price) of not taking care of it. Anything that weakens private property rights, such as nationalization or high taxes, tends to reduce incentives to do the socially responsible thing. Contracts are the lubrication for economic activity and wealth creation. Without contracts, all economic activity collapses to day-by-day negotiation and future activity commands a stiff penalty. Would you build a house, lend me money, or work for me if you could not be reasonably assured that I would honor the terms of our agreement? Money manipulation leading to inflation destroys the value of contracts. For example, I promise you $10,000 (which can now buy a small car) for three carloads of May 1993 potatoes. Suppose, in the interim, Congress inflates the currency so that $10,000 can no longer buy the car. Will you honor your end of the deal?

When all is said and done, it is free people with free minds that account for the creation of wealth. Free people and free minds permit us to escape nature's stingy grip. Because of technological advances, one farmer's output can feed thousands. Computers save millions of hours, dollars, and perhaps lives. Plus, these valuable machines are getting cheaper and better all the time. You name me one thing that government does that's getting cheaper. If you are not a staunch defender of free exchange, the sanctity of contracts, private property, and the right to earn, then you're for impoverishment of your fellow man.

Corruption of Language

March 10, 1993

Totalitarianism requires corruption of language and concepts. Tyrannical regimes call themselves "People's Democratic Republics"; indoctrination is called "reeducation"; genocidal murder is called "ethnic cleansing" or "racial purity"; dogma is called "enlightenment," ad nauseam. Let's look at similar corruption in our country.

"Those who've been blessed ought to give something back." That's emotionally appealing but deceitful. For the most part, people with high incomes have produced valuable services for their fellow man.

Sam Walton, founder of Walmart, Bill Gates, founder of Microsoft, and singer Michael Jackson provided services deemed highly valuable by their fellow men who voluntarily paid for those services. Incomes earned by these men stand as unambiguous proof that they served their fellow man. As such they've met their social obligations. So have grocery clerks, mechanics, and pharmacists in varying degrees.

In contrast, a thief truly should "give something back" because he's taken and has given nothing in return. We have it backward. Productive people (the rich), like Walton and Gates, are held up to social ridicule, while thieves, bums, and other social parasites are shown passion and concern and have become society's mascots.

"People have a right to food, decent housing, and medical care." That's a stupid statement. A right is something that exists simultaneously among people. My right to speech, religion, and move about freely imposes no positive obligation on you. My exercising these rights in no way diminishes your rights to the same. You have the "negative" obligation of noninterference.

So-called rights to food, housing, and medical care are something entirely different. In order to deliver on a "right" to food, housing, and medical care, government must burden others with the obligation to provide the same. As a consequence, those burdened are forced to have less food, housing, and medical care. If this lame notion of rights were applied to free speech, freedom of religion and movement, you'd be obliged to provide me with an auditorium, church, and plane fare. A better term for what we call rights nowadays is *wishes*.

Sensitivity is another corrupted term. Essentially, it means don't criticize, be judgmental, or call things what they are. Criticizing deadly homosexual lifestyles, flunking a student for poor performance, or acknowledging that women tend to be physically weaker than men or that black performance on standardized tests is lower than whites qualify one for charges of insensitivity and as a candidate for mandatory reeducation. In some cases, it has led to school expulsion or loss of promotions and jobs.

Then there's meaningless language to avoid the truth. How about "exceptional" child? I don't know if I want one around me. Would you want a "differently enabled" person to operate on you? You just don't know. My physician is an excellent internist but a poor economist and basketball player, making him differently enabled. How about a Native

American? Being born here, I am. "It goes by your roots, Williams, you are African American," you say. That poses a problem. There are Americans born Afrikaners and Egyptians. Are they African Americans as well?

John Milton predicted, "When language in common use in any country becomes irregular and depraved, it is followed by their ruin and degradation." Case closed just in case you're puzzled by our national decline.

Smart Economic Policy?

APRIL 21, 1993

Because of Japan's import restrictions on foreign goods, Japanese citizens pay $53 for jeans that cost us $32. A spark plug costs them $8.60; we can get one for $1.69. They pay $2,000 for a laser printer that costs us $1,100. So what should we do in response to Japan's restrictionist policies? Trade restrictionists, like Representative Richard Gephardt, advise that because Japan and other countries force their own citizens to pay higher prices, we should retaliate with restrictions that force Americans to pay higher prices as well. In other words, because Japan's trade restrictions force its citizens to pay $8.60 for a spark plug, Congress should punish Japan by adopting a policy that forces Americans to pay the same. We won't hear a congressman put it that way because his stupidity would be apparent to all. Instead, you'll hear such terms as *fair trade, antidumping,* and *voluntary restraints.* No matter how it's put, the bottom line is higher prices for us.

How about all those charlatans and quacks telling us we should have a government-managed health care system like the Canadians? I could bore you with all kinds of horror tales about Canada's health care, but I'm just going to give you a tiny morsel to ponder. If you visit hospitals in Rochester, New York, Minneapolis, Seattle, Detroit, and other cities close to Canada, you'll see many Canadian patients. In contrast, if you visit Montreal, Toronto, Windsor, and Vancouver hospitals, you are not likely to see American patients. I'm going to respect your intelligence and allow you to reach your own conclusion about the meaning of that observation. There's another Canada-related matter we might consider as we ponder Clinton's suggestion to regulate our drug industry. Canadian drug companies have not developed one major drug in the past half century. Sixty-two percent of all drug development happens in our country. If I had something against sick people, I'd call for socialized medicine.

Clinton has called for higher "sin" taxes for cigarettes and alcoholic beverages, saying their use creates a further burden on an already overburdened health care system. If burdens to the health care system are the new tax standard, why single out cigarettes and booze? Why not a salt tax? After all, salt consumption is a contributor to hypertension; plus, there's no dietary reason for adding salt to food. Then there's butter, sugar, margarine, steak, pies, cookies, and chocolates. Their unwise use leads to obesity, cholesterol-clogged arteries, and kidney disorders, all of which burden our health care system. Clinton might propose a lifestyle tax. We know there's a strong relationship between homosexual conduct and AIDS, which is also a great burden on our health care system. So maybe there should be a homosexual tax. For promiscuous heterosexuals, we might enact a "Magic Johnson tax." You see the point. Using sin and indiscretion as a justification, we could tax anything, even something you enjoy.

Secretly, Congress is talking about raising taxes on inherited wealth. How stupid can it be? If it raises taxes on inherited wealth, people will respond by creating and passing on less wealth to their heirs. Or they might find ingenious ways to avoid the tax in ways that increase disrespect for laws and are devastating to capital formation and hence future wealth.

Here's my approach to any new policy, except those cutting spending. First, it's probably not good for the country. Second, we should try it out on New Jersey to see whether it works before applying it to the other forty-nine states. And third, there should be an expiration date for any new laws, requiring reenactment after two years.

Welfare Kings and Queens

JUNE 16, 1993

Everybody knows about those welfare queens for whom we toil under
the congressional threat of fines, imprisonment, or, if we resist too
vehemently, death. If you don't believe there's coercion, just deduct
your per capita share of queen-support money from your 1040 tax
form. You may be surprised to know that welfarism knows no sex
and, for that matter, no income class. We have welfare kings who put
welfare queens to shame.

The National Wool Act of 1954 updated an earlier World War II
subsidy program for wool and mohair. Wool used to be considered a
strategic material because soldiers needed woolen clothing. With the
end of the war and the introduction of synthetic fibers, wool and
mohair fell off the military's list of strategic materials. But no big
thing. Congress instructs the U.S. Department of Agriculture to continue making welfare payments, now at $180 million a year, to sheep
and angora ranchers. In 1992, the Agriculture Department's office in
Rocksprings, Texas, issued $5.2 million in checks to sheep and mo-
hair ranchers. According to Sharon LaFraniere, staff writer for the
Washington Post, national weekly edition (4/12/93), Rocksprings's
top ten recipients collected between $90,000 and $340,000 apiece.
Two percent of the program's "welfarees" receive 54 percent of the
handouts.

Instead of eliminating this rich man's welfare, President Clinton's
budget proposes capping those payments at $50,000 per rancher. But
sheep and mohair ranchers, just like the welfare queens who use mul-
tiple names and addresses to get fatter checks, know the way around
caps. The ranchers, as they've done in the past, simply divide their
ranch among family members, making each eligible for the handout.
In this time of "concern" about budget deficits, why doesn't Clinton
just propose eliminating this costly, useless program? It turns out that
Representatives E ("Kika") de la Garza and Charles W. Stenholm are
powerful Democrats from Texas, a state that receives 86 percent of
mohair payments and 26 percent of wool payments. If Clinton alien-

ates these men, he won't be able to count on their votes for tax increases, support for government-sponsored pornographic art, or homosexuals in the military.

It'd be unfair to give the impression that only ranchers are fleecing us. Led by Archer-Daniel-Midland's multimillionaire CEO Wayne Andreas, the ethanol industry has received $7 billion in federal handouts since 1980. Senator Robert Dole, a Republican from Kansas, is the chief procurer for this handout. You say, "Clinton can't count on Dole for support, how come he doesn't ice the ethanol industry welfare?" That question shows how little you understand the inner workings of Washington. Clinton, Democrats, and other Washington insiders can count on Wayne Andreas for political contributions, junkets, and, if you're friendly enough, cheap condos.

Then there's a bank you've never heard of that Congress created for other welfare kings—the Export-Import Bank. Former Office of Management and Budget director David Stockman called it "food stamps for the rich." Congress created it to funnel our earnings into big businesses to the tune of $4 billion a year. In the past decade, 70 percent of Export-Import loans have gone to fewer than twenty corporations, including Boeing, Westinghouse, and General Motors. Just so you don't think college students are the only government loan deadbeats, in 1990, the Export-Import Bank stood ready to lose $5 billion. That's 40 percent of its outstanding loans and loan guarantees.

In this time of debt and deficit emergency, you ought to write or call the president and your congressman and ask why these wasteful programs exist. I guarantee that the letter coming back will be a lie.

Assorted Nonsense Update

DECEMBER 1, 1993

The average American hasn't time to keep up with all the asinine goings-on in the name of the environment, fairness, and sensitivity. You won't learn about it on the six o'clock news and that's where Williams comes in.

On August 3, 1993, Representative Phil Crane (R-Ill.) invited the Christian Action Network to display in the House of Representatives art funded through the National Endowment for the Arts (NEA). The exhibit included the homoerotic art of Robert Mapplethorpe and Joel Witkin featuring stretched testicles, a bare-breasted female Christ painting, and a fat nude holding two fetuses. Within hours, Representatives Rostenkowski and Foley ordered the exhibit removed. It appears that while Rostenkowski and Foley vote to support NEA-funded filth, they don't want a public display of your tax dollars at work.

The enviro-Nazis must feel good. According to *Access to Energy* (July 1993), the U.S. Air Force reacted to the Environmental Protection Agency ban on chlorofluorocarbons (CFCs) by replacing the cooling systems on its multiple-warhead nuclear intercontinental ballistic missiles. Thus, should there ever be a nuclear exchange, it will be an environmentally friendly event not threatening to the earth's ozone layer.

You might be wondering about all the crime in the nation's capital. Here's what may be part of the answer. According to the September 1993 *Mediawatch*, one out of every sixty-one Washington cops is currently under criminal indictment or has a case pending. Plus, there are affirmative-action policies whereby police exam scores are manipulated on the basis of race, sex, residency, and whether they went to D.C. schools. So, if you visit the nation's capital and happen to be confronted by a criminal, think twice before you run into the arms of a cop.

This is my thirteenth year at George Mason University, a university previously spared from Nazi-like brownshirts. But as with any disease, their contamination spreads. George Mason just came out with a brochure classifying what constitutes sexual discrimination and harassment. "Thinking that a homosexual might come on to you" or "jumping when a homosexual touches you on the arm" are listed among the forms of discrimination and harassment. Plus, "keeping a physical distance from someone because they are a known gay or lesbian" and "staring at two homosexuals holding hands" are also forbidden.

You ask, "Williams, what are you going to do?" It's business as usual with minor modifications. Because I think that women might come on to me, in the name of equality I must think that a homosexual might come on to me as well. After all, I'm a fairly handsome guy. I may call George Johnson, our president, to find out what is the politically correct physical distance one should be from anyone and extend the same courtesy to homosexuals. While I have his ear, I shall seek counsel on how long you can look at homosexuals holding hands, or otherwise physically connected, before it constitutes an illegal stare. If the president says to me you can't be more than thirteen and a half inches from someone—no problem. There's not even a problem if he tells me that looking for more than forty-seven seconds at physically connected homosexuals violates university policy. And even if it imposes a self-esteem burden, there's no problem being told I must not think homosexuals might come on to me. But I draw the line at touching. I do not play touching. Even though we've been married thirty-three years, my wife must gain permission before she touches me. In fact, she must verbally specify, in advance, where and in what manner she wishes to touch me.

End of update on insanity in America.